PSI SUCCESSFUL BUSINESS LIBRARY

Before You Go Into Business, Read This

Ira N. Nottonson

THE OASIS PRESS®
CENTRAL POINT, OREGON

Before You Go Into Business, Read This!
Published by The Oasis Press®/PSI Research
© 1998 by Ira N. Nottonson

The names appearing in the book representing business situations are not the names of people actually involved. The only exception to this is the name of Lisa Lecko, who is the author's daugter.

This publication is designed to provide accurate and authoritative information in regard to the subject matter covered. It is sold with the understanding that the author and publisher are not engaged in rendering legal, accounting, or other professional service. If legal advice or other expert assistance is required, the services of a competent professional person should be sought.

> *— from a declaration of principles jointly adopted by a committee of the American Bar Association and a committee of publishers.*

Cover design: Steven Eliot Burns

Please direct any comments, questions, or suggestions regarding this book to:
The Oasis Press®/PSI Research
Editorial Department
P.O. Box 3727
Central Point, Oregon 97502-0032
(541) 479-9464
(541) 476-1479 fax
info@psi-research.com e-mail

The Oasis Press® is a Registered Trademark of Publishing Services, Inc., an Oregon corporation doing business as PSI Research.

Library of Congress Cataloging-in-Publication Data
Nottonson, Ira N., 1933 –
    Before you go into business, read this! / Ira N. Nottonson.
    p. cm. – – (PSI successful business library)
    Includes index.
    ISBN 1-55571-481-1 (pbk.)
    1. New business enterprises – Handbooks; manuals, etc. 2. Small business – – Management – – Hanbooks, manuals, etc. I. Title. II. Series.
HD62.5.N69 1999
658.02'2––dc21
                                                                   99–10747
                                                                       CIP

Printed and bound in the United States of America
First Edition 10 9 8 7 6 5 4

 Printed on recycled paper when available.

Dedication

To those in the business marketplace who have the courage to
admit what they don't know, the willingness to apply what they know is right,
and the intelligence to recognize the difference.

About the Author

As an entrepreneur, Ira Nottonson has had extensive experience, including having owned his own advertising agency, publishing house, and television production company. At present, he acts in a consulting capacity specializing in the valuation of businesses and helping other entrepreneurs find the most direct route to success.

Ira is a Law Review Graduate of Boston College Law School and has practiced law in both Massachusetts and California. He has also participated in the corporate business/franchise community in a variety of capacities, including Chief Executive Officer of an American company as well as Managing Director of a British company. These businesses include NYSE and AMEX corporations, as well as a number of smaller companies, many of which are familiar images on the American business landscape, including: International House of Pancakes, Orange Julius of America, House of Pies, PIP Printing, PIP/UK (the British subsidiary of PIP Printing), Copper Family Family Restaurants, Love's Wood-Pit Barbeque Restaurants, the Bryman-Sawyer Schools, United Rent-All, and Big Red Q Quickprint Centers. As a member of the management committees of most of the above companies, he has been an integral part of the planning and implementation of basic business concepts.

He has published a variety of articles, which include such diverse subjects as:

> The Three Basic Principles of Leadership; Marketing: The Ultimate Tool for Competition; Competition and Complacency in the Marketplace; The Secret Formula for Buying and Selling a Business; Another View: Don't Start a New Business—Buy An Old One, and I'll Tell You Why; Franchising: Which Is David and Which Is Goliath?

In 1994, he published the book *The Secrets to Buying and Selling a Business,* which is now in its third edition. (Published by The Oasis Press/PSI/Research, Grants Pass, Oregon).

Mr. Nottonson is constantly traveling the country valuing businesses, advising companies on "how to reach the next plateau of success," and lecturing. At his home base in Boulder, Colorado, he teaches the FastTrac II Entrepreneur course (for people in business). This is sponsored by the Small Business Development Center at the Boulder Chamber of Commerce.

He can be reached at his phone and fax: 303-447-9672, or by email at irabizlaw@aol.com.

Foreword

The hardest part of being in business, if a person hasn't specifically gone to business school, is to understand the language of business. In all of the years that I have been a small business owner, a lender, and a business educator, I have not seen a comprehensive book that explains the basic elements of business in a language that everyone can understand...until now. Mr. Nottonson has drawn on his vast experience in dealing with businesses at all levels to take the mystery out of a language that is taken for granted by business service professionals and feared or misunderstood by small business owners.

Small business is the backbone of the American economy. Small businesses are started by individuals who are knowledgeable about a specific idea or product. Their ability to understand the marketing, financial, and legal aspects of operating a business, however, is often beyond their education or experience. *Before You Go Into Business, Read This!* will give the small business owner a realistic and understandable perspective of the language and concepts so necessary to profitably carry their product or service into the marketplace.

Smart business owners are those individuals who seeks out the professional in each field to bridge the gap between what they know and what they need to know. *Before You Go Into Business, Read This!* will also help the small business owner understand the necessary elements that need to be properly placed to build and ensure a successful business. Knowing and understanding these elements will enable the owner to choose the dynamic team of professionals so necessary for the success of any business endeavor.

A must read for business owners and professionals!

Marilynn Force
Director, Boulder Chamber Small Business Development Center
Adjunct Professor, Graduate MBA programs, Regis University
Adjunct Professor, Metropolitan State College Entrepreneurship Institute

Introduction

One significant purpose (if not the primary purpose) of this book is to ensure that the simple things are kept simple, that the complex things are converted to simple things, and that the "I don't understand" becomes "I didn't realize how simple it was."

As you deal with professionals, including—but not necessarily limited to—lawyers, accountants, insurance agents, and brokers of all types, you invariably find them using words and phrases you've never heard before. It is disconcerting to say the least, embarrassing in most cases and, at its worst, dangerous. You are often caused—or in some cases even "forced"—to make a serious business decision based on less than an adequate understanding of the elements on which your judgment will be predicated. This is definitely not acceptable!

There are many business terms that make you feel only a college professor can understand and operate a business. If this were so, only a small percentage of the great business marketplace would exist. But you must be careful not to dismiss certain basic concepts just because they "sound" complicated. The accountant speaks of profit and loss statements, cash flow projections, and balance sheets; the advertising professional speaks of demographic dichotomies; the lawyer speaks of rights of first refusal; the landlord refers to COLAs and percentage rents; and the vendor shows us one-page contracts with print so small you can't read it and, even if you could, it is not understandable to the layperson. What is this morass of words all about, and how do we make sense of it?

Many professionals have long since forgotten (if, indeed, they ever knew) how to communicate with their clientele. They are so used to speaking with their peers on a level of buzz words peculiar only to their respective professions that the import of their opinions and advice is often lost to the people who need it most—the client—you! You will note the doctor in Chapter 9, *Dealing with the Professionals* who uses "myocardial infarction" instead of saying "heart attack." If your professional cannot communicate with you so that you understand the problem, the analysis, and the solution—get another professional. Remember, nothing is so complex that it cannot be broken down into its component parts so that each part can be examined and understood. Then the parts can be put back together again and the picture becomes clear.

As you read some of these chapters, the language will be very simple for those of you who have already grappled with the concepts the words represent. Hopefully, it will at least be understandable to those of you who have not. The idea is for every reader to understand all of it. The sections on things like "retail" and "wholesale" are certainly simple enough. Chapter 3, *The Business Plan: Developing a Road Map,* as with certain other chapters, starts off with the simple method of laying out the format. You can, of course, make it as complex as you choose once you understand the basic format. Other chapters such as Chapter 21, *Legal Entities: A Simple Equation,* and the joint venture concept of borrowing or selling equity positions in your business, Chapter 10, *More on Investors and Partners,* will require a second reading for those of you who have not yet addressed these subjects.

You should enjoy learning the things you didn't know and forgive the writer for the oversimplification of those things you already know. You should feel good about the fact that the things you know are the things that others are just beginning to learn.

Ira N. Nottonson

Table of Contents

1

The Financial Picture

Starting or operating a business should not require an MBA (Master Degree in Business Administration) from Stanford University. It should not even require a college accounting course. As the old saying goes, "if it were that difficult, only a very few would be doing it." In fact, if this were true, most of the small businesses that now support the country would be absent from the business landscape.

Basically simple concepts

Double entry accounting, general ledger, profit and loss statement, cash flow projections, and balance sheet are very intimidating names for basically simple concepts. They all stem from the three fundamental financial principles of operating a business: How much did it cost me? How much did I sell it for? And, how much is left? This is, literally, the beginning of the game of financial bookkeeping. Don't let the language of the professionals intimidate you.

Business is broken down into a variety of categories. Three basic categories are: manufacturing, service, and distribution. The business of selling a service would include everything from washing windows and cutting grass to a dentist fixing teeth or a lawyer giving advice on a business problem.

The business of distributing product would include selling lemonade and cookies on the street corner and selling automobiles or clothing. The business of manufacturing includes buildings, computers, and airplanes. Manufacturing is a good place to start because you have to actually "create" your product and then you have to figure out how to sell it to the ultimate customer.

The manufacturing process

Let's say you are in the business of making wooden deer (a simplistic, block design replica of a miniature deer) to be placed, more likely than not, on the front lawns of people's homes. The size of each product will vary and, to a great degree, price will be based on size and intricacy of design. For the moment, consider a wooden deer that can fit into a 1 foot cube; i.e., 1 foot high by 1 foot wide by 1 foot deep. To manufacture the deer, you will need:

 a. Transportation to search out the wood or to find a place to buy the wood.
 b. Tools to cut, shape, and finish the wood. The first products will be "rough cut," which will not require finishing tools or finishing ability.
 c. Glue to manufacture the finished product.

If the wood is handy (easily obtainable without cost), you can eliminate the cost factor in a. above. You then go to the hardware store to find the right tools. The first approach is to buy only the tools you need and use your own labor for the rest of the manufacturing process. Later, you will buy more expensive tools to save labor. This is called reinvesting your profit to build a better and less labor-intensive manufacturing capability.

The glue to finalize the finished product can be made (see your local library—"how to" books) or it can be purchased. At the early stages the best plan is to make whatever you can and save your dollars for the things you can't make or for the emergencies you were not able to anticipate. It is recommended that most small businesses be started using as little money as possible consistent with the elements necessary to start and build the business properly. For a more advanced discussion of this concept, see Chapter 3, *The Business Plan*. Always remember: Be sure you have all the necessary tools and raw materials before you start the business.

Imagine you are using a checkbook to operate your business. First, you put in some money so you'll be able to write checks. This is called the investment in the business. (We will talk about the method of raising the money from various sources in Chapter 2, *Getting the Money*.)

To start with, you will deposit $200 in the bank. Now you will have to write a check for $38 for tools at the hardware store. This leaves $162 in the bank. ($200 originally deposited minus $38 for tools equals $162.)

		RECORD ALL CHARGES OR CREDITS THAT AFFECT YOUR ACCOUNT						
NUMBER	DATE	DESCRIPTION OF TRANSACTION	PAYMENT/ DEBIT (-)	✓ T	FEE (IF ANY) (-)	DEPOSIT/ CREDIT (+)	BALANCE $	
		Deposit from savings				200 00		
							200 00	
		Tools	38 00				38 00	
							162 00	

Marketing and advertising

You manufacture the product, perhaps 10 of them. By imitating the simple product in the picture (and, after making some normal mistakes—wasting some time, some energy, and some raw materials) you should be able to replicate the deer for sale. Now you must examine your market and decide the best way to advertise your product. (This will be discussed in more detail in Chapter 13, *Marketing and Advertising*.)

Your marketing research should tell you that your product will sell more easily to people in single family homes—who have lawns and porches—than to apartment dwellers, who have limited exterior space. Later you will examine diversification and expansion of your product line. For example, you might develop "miniatures" for apartment dwellers. To determine if this is a good idea, take a look at your marketplace. See what others are selling. Always examine the competitive aspect of your market. This will often dictate the direction your diversification will take.

Your advertising programs will probably be labor intensive at the beginning, as opposed to spending money on brochures or mailers or leaflets, which cost you for paper, printing, and distribution. With a product of this nature, "show and tell" will probably be your best advertising approach. This means that you will probably "carry" a finished product door to door to generate interest and sales.

Pricing your product

The price of your product is certainly problematic at the outset. A good suggestion is always to "check your competition." Find out what the stores are selling it (or a comparable product) for. If you find the price is $25 and the quality of your product is comparable, then you have a good starting point. Since you are new in the business you might make an initial downward price adjustment to make your first sales. It's always nice to know your efforts can actually be financially rewarding. It helps to build your confidence, and confidence is one of the key factors in the success of any business. You must believe your business venture will succeed. (See Chapter 4, *Looking in the Mirror*.) But be careful that your "downward price adjustment in order to make your first sales" does not become unreasonable. There is a potential backlash to take into consideration.

Take the case of Charlie Bainbridge. To guarantee his initial sales, Charlie priced his goods well below the market price. In fact, his selling price was actually less than his cost of production. He sold his initial inventory, but when he went back to his customers for reorders—at a substantial increase in price—the customers stopped buying his product. You must be able to make a profit on your goods or services or your business will not survive. Remember the old business adage: "You can't lose a nickel on every sale and make it up in volume."

If you start selling at $15 and you sell your entire inventory—all 10 products—you will have $150 to deposit into your business account. Now, looking at your cash position, you will note that you have $312 in the bank.

		RECORD ALL CHARGES OR CREDITS THAT AFFECT YOUR ACCOUNT					
NUMBER	DATE	DESCRIPTION OF TRANSACTION	PAYMENT/ DEBIT (-)	✓ T	FEE (IF ANY) (-)	DEPOSIT/ CREDIT (+)	BALANCE $
							162 00
		Money received from sales				150 00	150 00
							312 00

Going back to basics: a) the tools to manufacture the product cost you $38. This is a nonrecurring expense, by the way. That is, you only have to buy the tools once—you can use them over and over again. The $200 initial investment minus the $38 for tools equals $162 plus the $150 from sales equals $312. It's time to convert your checking account concept to a profit and loss statement to better understand the long-term perspective.

> Profit and Loss Statement
> Sales: $150
> Expenses: $ 38
> Gross profit: $112

You sold your products for $150; your costs have been exclusively for tools at $38; you can see that you have made a gross profit of $112. This is the beginning of your business. (See Chapter 12, *Understanding Your Income Statement.*)

A little bit about taxes

All businesses in the United States are supposed to pay taxes on "profit." The question is, just what is the "profit?" For tax purposes, it is not $112. The government allows you to deduct the expenses necessary to operate your business before your "profit" is determined and taxed. Any money you spent for bus fare, or a new bicycle tire, or a taxicab ride, or gasoline for a car, or salaries—including your own—that was "incurred" in the operation of your business is "deductible." In Chapter 12, you will see that expenses "incurred" might not be the same as expenses "paid"; this involves the difference between cash accounting and accrual accounting.

Depreciation

Occasionally, you may break a saw, which has to be replaced, or a blade may become dull and need to be sharpened. The "replacement" may cause you to examine "depreciation," and the sharpening may cause you to examine "maintenance and repair expense" as other categories on your financial paperwork. (See Chapter 20, *Running a Business for Profit.*) The cost of sharpening or replacing your handsaw, a relatively minor cost, is a deductible business expense in the year you spend the money. If you have to *replace* a power saw because it breaks or *replace* your bicycle with a new one, a relatively substantial cost, you can take a tax deduction. This is known as depreciation. Since the government may say your bicycle should last five years (they have many arbitrary judgments like this), you can deduct one-fifth of the price of your bicycle each year as a business expense, even though you may not buy a new one until the end of the five years or longer.

In this way, you have actually "saved" the price of the bicycle during these five years by taking a business deduction each year for five years. It's a part of your profit on which you have not paid tax. For example, if the bicycle costs $250, you can take a $50 business deduction each year (one-fifth of $250), and when you're ready to buy the new bicycle at the end of the five years, you will have theoretically "saved" enough money to do that.

Keep in mind that depreciation is known as a noncash item. In other words, even though you've deducted it to lower your taxable income, you don't really take the depreciation in cash. It is a paper transaction only and, in turn, it is only a theoretical savings. You could, of course, take the cash and put it into a savings account for the time when you really need to replace the bicycle. Most people don't do this because the deduction is designed to be a tax savings, not normally a real cash savings. This is known as "depreciating" the asset over its legal life span. Keep in mind, you don't *have* to buy a new bicycle at the end of five years. The bicycle may last ten years or it may last only three years.

If it lasts longer than five years, you can only take a deduction for the $50 per year for five years because you will have "fully depreciated" the cost; that is, you will have taken the maximum deduction for tax purposes (the full price of the bicycle). If the bicycle lasts only three years, you will have taken a deduction of only $150 (representing less than the original cost) but you can add the balance of $100 to the cost of a new bicycle, creating a new "basis" and continuing a new "depreciation process" in this way.

Original purchase price of bicycle: $250.
Depreciation at $50 per year based on a "life" of five years.
Total depreciation taken over three years: $150.
Balance of depreciation not yet taken: $100.
Cost of new bicycle: $250.

Add to this price the balance of depreciation not yet taken: $100.
This equals $350, which now represents the "basis" of the new bicycle.
You may now start your depreciation all over again with a "basis" (beginning figure for depreciation purposes) of $350.
If the theoretical life of this new bicycle is five years, you can take one-fifth of $350 as depreciation: $70 per year.
Keep in mind that there are many different formulas for handling depreciation. (See your accountant regarding how and when to apply the various formulas.)

A question of semantics...or taxes

If the item to be replaced is comparatively inexpensive, then you won't take the deduction over a period of time by depreciating it. You can take the entire cost of the replacement item at one time—in the year of the purchase. This is known as "expensing" the cost of the item instead of depreciating it. This is a better position, if you can assume it, because it lowers the amount of the final profit on which you will be paying taxes in any given year.

For example, if you expensed the cost of the bicycle instead of depreciating it, you would deduct $250 as a business expense in one year rather than the $50 from the previous example. If your profit would have been $1,000 *before* using the bicycle as a business deduction, depreciation of $50 would leave a taxable income of $950. On the other hand, an expense of $250 would leave a taxable income of only $750. Quite a difference in the tax bite! What will happen during the next taxable year if you have already expensed the bicycle in the previous year? You won't be able to take *any* deduction because you've already used it up. As you can see, long-term thinking can be a business advantage. Be sure you examine this kind of problem with your accounting professional.

Calendar versus fiscal

Most businesses work on a "calendar year" basis—January 1 through December 31. This is considered your tax year—the same period on which your personal income tax is computed. In other words, you are taxed on the income you earned during this calendar year. And you may deduct your expenses incurred during this calendar year.

The government also allows you to use a different year as long as it includes a full 12 months. This is usually done for bookkeeping or tax purposes. For example, you may use July 1 through June 30. This is known as a "fiscal year" instead of a calendar year. In other words, a fiscal year can begin at the start of any month and concludes exactly 12 months later. When you get to Chapter 21, *Legal Entities*, you will note that the fiscal year is reexamined.

Key points

- You must believe that your business venture will be a success.
- Be sure you have the necessary tools and materials before you start your business.
- Always examine and understand the competitive aspect of your market.
- Price your product to be competitive. Sales develop confidence in your business.
- Make sure you understand all the possible deductions before you pay your taxes.

Worksheet

- Name some businesses based on the manufacturing of goods.
- When would you use the "show and tell" method of advertising?
- Name one way to determine a starting price for your product.
- What kind of business deductions can you take before you compute the taxes payable on your profit?
- What is the difference between depreciation and expensing?
- What is the difference between a calendar year and a fiscal year?

FINANCIAL STORY BOARD
For the Proverbial Widget Manufacturing Company
(a little more complicated than the wooden deer enterprise)

1. Begin your financial "story board" with the simplest concept.
   Deposit: From personal finances or borrowed money—$1,000
   Expenses: Business certificate for a new business; lawyer's fees, accountant's fees
   (see Chapter 9; *Dealing with Professionals*); office supplies, etc.—$800
   Balance: $200

RECORD ALL CHARGES OR CREDITS THAT AFFECT YOUR ACCOUNT

NUMBER	DATE	DESCRIPTION OF TRANSACTION	PAYMENT/ DEBIT (-)	✓ T	FEE (IF ANY) (-)	DEPOSIT/ CREDIT (+)	BALANCE $
		Deposit from savings				1000 00	
							1000 00
		Expenses	800 00				800 00
							200 00

2. After "developing" a business plan for investors (see Chapter 3, *The Business Plan*), you have succeeded in obtaining $10,000 in additional working capital (money to operate the business). Some of this was given as a "loan" and some of it was given as an investment (see Chapter 10, *More on Investors and Partners*)

   Now, you have:
   Previous balance: $200
   Additional deposit: $10,000
   New balance: $10,200

RECORD ALL CHARGES OR CREDITS THAT AFFECT YOUR ACCOUNT

NUMBER	DATE	DESCRIPTION OF TRANSACTION	PAYMENT/ DEBIT (-)	✓ T	FEE (IF ANY) (-)	DEPOSIT/ CREDIT (+)	BALANCE $ 200 00
		Additional deposit				10000 00	10000 00
							10200 00

3. After developing your prototype and getting some products manufactured for sale, you are ready to get into the marketplace.

   Now, you have:
   Previous balance: $10,200 (carried from #2 above)
   New expenses, i.e., the "cost of manufacturing": $3,000 (100 units @ $30 each)
   New balance: $7,200

RECORD ALL CHARGES OR CREDITS THAT AFFECT YOUR ACCOUNT

NUMBER	DATE	DESCRIPTION OF TRANSACTION	PAYMENT/ DEBIT (-)	✓ T	FEE (IF ANY) (-)	DEPOSIT/ CREDIT (+)	BALANCE $ 10200 00
		Manufacturing expenses	3000 00				3000 00
							7200 00

4. It is time for you to advertise your product for sale. This will require $2,000.

   Now, you have:
   Balance (from #3 above): $7,200.
   New expenses, i.e., cost of advertising: $2,000
   New balance: $5,200

RECORD ALL CHARGES OR CREDITS THAT AFFECT YOUR ACCOUNT

NUMBER	DATE	DESCRIPTION OF TRANSACTION	PAYMENT/ DEBIT (-)	✓ T	FEE (IF ANY) (-)	DEPOSIT/ CREDIT (+)	BALANCE $ 7200 00
		Advertising expenses	2000 00				2000 00
							5200 00

5. Sales of $8,000 (100 units @ $80 each) are generated—four times the dollars spent for advertising.

   Now, you have:
   Balance (from #4 above): $5,200
   Sales: (deposits) $8,000
   Balance: $13,200

The previous steps constitute the formation stage of the business.

RECORD ALL CHARGES OR CREDITS THAT AFFECT YOUR ACCOUNT

NUMBER	DATE	DESCRIPTION OF TRANSACTION	PAYMENT/ DEBIT (-)	✓ T	FEE (IF ANY) (-)	DEPOSIT/ CREDIT (+)	BALANCE $ 5200 00
		Deposit from sales				8000 00	8000 00
							13200 00

6. This stage is the beginning of "the business." This represents the *cash position* of your business: money in, money out. Now you should consider the "profit and loss" aspect of your business. Each month should now show sales minus expenses equals profit. This is the beginning of your profit and loss statement.

   Sales in February: $8,000
   Advertising in January: $2,000
   Cost of manufacturing (in January): $3,000

Total expenses: $5,000
Profit for the January/February period: $3,000

Your product is a success in the marketplace.

You should note that money is normally invested in advertising to generate sales, just as the cost of manufacturing of the product must necessarily precede the sale of the product. Note the expenses in January leading to sales in February. This is one of the reasons why you need "working capital" (money to operate the business). Even though the business is a "success," you will need to spend the dollars (for example, on advertising and manufacturing) *before* you can sell the product and enjoy the profit.

7. You then decide to do two things:

A. You want to spend more money for advertising, hoping that sales will still be four times the dollars spent for advertising. This would mean that, if you double your advertising (from $2,000 per month to $4,000 per month), you should double your sales (from $8,000 per month to $16,000 per month). *Although the theory is simple enough, your experience in business will ultimately tell you that such an equation will not necessarily hold true.*

B. You want to find a way to save money on manufacturing because you are making more product and, theoretically, you ought to be able to take advantage of quantity discounts when buying the component parts or raw materials that make up the final product you are selling. You save 20% on the production cost of each unit, which equals $6 per unit. *This also is logical enough in theory but, again, this "savings" depends on many factors other than just quantity.*

So, your business structure will change to something more like this:

You spend $4,000 in advertising per month.
You sell 200 units per month with a retail value of $16,000.
Your manufacturing cost is $4,800. Remember, your cost was originally $30 per unit. You manufactured 100 units at $30 per unit for a total cost of $3,000. Now, your cost per unit (because of the 20% savings in quantity discount for your component parts and raw material) is $24 per unit—a savings of $6 per unit—which brings your manufacturing cost for the 200 units sold this month to $4,800.

You now have:
Advertising for February: $4,000
Manufacturing for February: $4,800

Sales for March: $16,000
Profit for March: $7,200

Profit and Loss Statement—Year to Date
Sales: $16,000
Expenses of sale: $8,800
Profit: $7,200

You will notice that some of the items on your Profit and Loss Statement are noted for February and others for March. In addition to the above explanation (expenditures preceding sales), you will need to understand the difference between an income statement kept on a "cash basis" as opposed to one carried on an "accrual basis." See Chapter 12, Understanding Your Income Statement.

Some other considerations that have been avoided to keep the concept simple include the following: packaging (cost of personnel and boxes); shipping (whether by UPS or other delivery system); warehousing (if the manufacturer to whom responsibility for the production of the product has been allocated does not "drop ship"* to your customers); and creative and graphic arts aspect of the advertising being used in the media (whether by radio, newspaper, television, brochures, or other means—see Chapter 13, *Marketing and Advertising.*)

It is now time to consider a variety of changes to the business. You have succeeded in developing a product that has a salable position in the marketplace. You have proven that a monthly investment of $8,800 can generate sales of $16,000, leaving you with a profit of $7,200.

Now, you have:
 Sales: $16,000
 Cost of product (which includes your basic expense of advertising and manufac-
  turing) of $8,800, or 55% of your retail selling price.
 A profit of $7,200, or 45% of your retail sales.

As you watch your business grow, you will want to maintain a careful surveillance of the cost percentages—particularly cost of product (which will eventually be broken down to include many other items, such as salaries, rent, telephone, etc.) and your profit percentage to be sure the business is not costing more than it is delivering.

You must now move into a somewhat more complex business position.

---

* Drop shipping is when the manufacturer ships the product directly to the customer

In #2 above, you recall that you generated $10,000 of additional working capital (money to operate the business) from outside sources. Part of this was an "investment," for which you agreed to give the investors 5% of the profit.

Balance sheet

Another part of this "working capital" was "a loan," which you agreed to pay back. There are many ways to return this loan: monthly payments with interest on the unpaid principal; monthly payments of interest only with the entire principal payable at the end of the agreed term; or any number of other methods by which you could have agreed to return the loan with interest for the period during which you were privileged to "use" it. For purposes of this exercise, you will agree to pay the interest monthly on the unpaid principal and to repay the entire principal amount at the end of five years. This loan is evidenced by a promissory note and the interest has been agreed to be 10%. The monthly payments on the $5,000 will be $41.66 ($5,000 times 10% equals $500 per year, divided by 12 months equals $41.66 per month).

You will carry this $5,000 loan on another financial format known as a "balance sheet," and you will reflect each monthly payment of interest on your income statement (your profit and loss statement). The balance sheet explains in financial terms the three elements that show a picture of the long-term stability of the company: total assets (positive value); total liabilities (negative obligations) and owner's equity (the net value of the business). A good rule to start thinking about is assets minus liabilities equals owner's equity. This will be examined in future chapters.

As your business grows, you realize you need to spend additional dollars. This may be for any number of reasons. Some of these other more sophisticated elements that now need to be considered are:

1. You may want to incorporate to limit some of your personal liability with respect to certain business obligations. See Chapter 21, *Legal Entities.*
2. You may want to hire an accountant or buy a computer and the appropriate software to handle your books and records as well as preparation for your taxes. See Chapter 16, *Improving Your Business.*
3. You may have started the business as a "home based business" and you may now find a need for regarding your customers in a more business-like atmosphere. This will require you to lease a business facility and, ultimately, perhaps to buy your own building. You may also want to perform part of the manufacturing function yourself (instead of outsourcing), in which case you will need a facility in which to establish such a program. You may also need a business facility for

warehousing if your manufacturer, as mentioned earlier, is not drop shipping to your customers. See Chapter 20, *Running a Business for Profit*.

4. You may want to hire office personnel, manufacturing people, and salespeople as your business expands and as you find it more and more difficult to handle all these functions by yourself. In this context, you may be looking for paid personnel or, in some cases, for a partner.

5. You may decide to buy or lease equipment that can help your manufacturing capability. Sometimes equipment can make a better product, making it more competitive, and sometimes equipment can make more product in less time.

All of the above options require money. Sometimes you can bootstrap your growth by using "profit dollars" for such expansion. Sometimes you will need additional investors or partners to put in the dollars in anticipation of an accelerated growth program. Sometimes you will have to sell part of your ownership in the business to get the additional money. See Chapter 10, *More on Investors and Partners*.

The last thing that ought to be mentioned is the fact that the sales, expenses, and profit of the above example need to have a caution attached. Although it is possible to have a business grow in such a fashion that would be very exciting to its owner as well as to its investors, such is not often the case. Investors understand this.

More often than not, a new business will show a loss in the early days because of necessary expenses that are not covered by sales. The business may actually "go into the hole" for a while until the sales "catch up" with the investment required to generate those sales. Don't be concerned if this looks like your picture. Just be sure your "time line" for growth is consistent with the money you have available to reach that point. Careful planning will always be the key!

This chapter, with its Financial Story Board and the various explanations, is designed to touch on a variety of items that will become more apparent and more defined as the book progresses. They have not been fully explained here, for the most part, since you only need to reflect on certain aspects of them at this time. It's very much like looking at a watch. You only need to know how to tell the time; you don't need to know how the watch is made.

Key points and worksheet

For the moment, it is important for you to merely recognize some of the financial elements you will eventually need to understand more fully as you start and grow your business.

Some of these elements are:

the *cash position* of the business...the *profit and loss statement* (also known as the Income Statement)...*depreciating versus expensing* of costs and expenses...the difference between *expenses incurred and expenses paid*...leading to the difference between *cash accounting and accrual accounting...money spent in anticipation of sales...the basis on which taxes are assessed* after taking the appropriate business deductions...the need for *working capital* (money to operate the business)

How many of them do you recognize?

Do you understand why it is essential that you have a professional accountant on your business team?

When do you think would be a good time to get to know a good professional?

2

Getting the Money

Whatever the business...

Whether you are starting a lemonade stand at age eight or starting a consulting practice based on a lifetime of experience at age eighty, you will need start-up capital: the money necessary to fund the business, enabling it to buy raw material, build an office capability, rent premises, or acquire inventory. This may be as simple as a dozen lemons, a cup of sugar, a container to pour from, some paper cups, a box to use as a stand, and a sign to capture the attention of your potential customers. On the other hand, it may be as complex as a computer, computer software, a telephone, a fax machine, a telephone answering machine, a photocopier, paper, stationery, business cards, and dedicated telephone lines for the modem, the fax, and the telephone. Instead of the sign to get the attention of passing traffic, you'll also need a brochure or other method of advertising your services.

If you start a retail business, you'll need a place of business and an inventory. If you start a service business, you'll need equipment and possibly transportation. Whatever the venture may be, you will need money as working capital—the money necessary to convert the business idea into a functioning business. One of the biggest reasons for failure in the start-up of a new business or the takeover of an existing business is the lack of adequate working capital. This is good enough reason to build a business plan that shows just what dollars are going to allow the business to achieve certain plateaus during its growth period. See Chapter 3, *The Business Plan,* for a more detailed explanation.

Look in your pocket

Since most people will not have the same vision you do for the success of your business, it may be difficult to get them to loan you money or invest in your business. The first place to look for money will be your own pocket. If you have enough of your own money to start the business, you will not have to share the profits with anyone. If you don't have enough of your own money and you need to borrow some, you will at least be showing people you have enough confidence in your business idea to put your own money at risk. After all, why would anyone want to risk his or her money on your idea if you are not willing to risk your own?

The joint venture

Every new business venture needs start-up capital. Every existing business that is purchased requires working capital. Sometimes the money is used to buy equipment or raw materials. Sometimes the money is used to hire the people you need to help build the business—including yourself. Apart from finding it in your own bank account, there are really two basic ways to get money for a business venture. You can *borrow* it with the intention of paying it back someday with interest for the period of time you've used it. Or you can *sell a part of your business* in return for the money a person invests. This is called giving an equity position to the investor. There are, of course, combinations of these two concepts—a little borrowing and a little equity selling.

Variations on the theme

There are many variations on these concepts. As the business becomes more sophisticated, a lender may have *options* to take an equity position (an opportunity to acquire an interest) in the business at a later time when the company has proven itself successful. Sometimes this opportunity is built into the concept of the company "going public." This happens when the company actually sells part of its stock to outsiders who invest in the public marketplace, for example, on the stock exchanges. But these positions are for a later time when the simple business goes beyond simple concepts. On the simple side, it is fair to remain with the two basics; borrowing, or sharing your profit with a third party who has invested on the basis of taking an equity position in your business.

Borrowing

The problem with borrowing is that you have to pay the money back with interest. You can borrow it for a period of time, say, one year. Your agreement can be that you'll pay it all back plus interest at the end of the year. You can also pay "interest only" on the note during the year and pay the entire principal (the entire borrowed amount) at the end of the year. Or you can agree to pay portions of it back on a monthly basis with the accrued (earned) interest each month, so that at the end of the year the borrowed money and the interest are all paid. This is called "amortizing the loan." Of course, there are even variations on these basic approaches.

Security for the loan

When people loan money to other people, they usually want some assurance that the money will be paid back. However, in the event they do not get paid as anticipated, they would like to know that they can depend on another method to ensure the return of their money. They will usually ask for some security, which will serve as an alternative in the event you cannot repay the loan. If you don't repay the loan, they will keep the security, which could be a car, a house, or other real estate or personal property that has a substantial market value, and which they can relatively easily convert to dollars.

Investing

The aspect of sharing your ownership position with someone who has money to invest has some positives and negatives, just as borrowing does. The positive side is that you won't have to return the money to the investor because the money has been invested, not loaned. The negative side is that the investor will have the right to "look over your shoulder" as you operate the business. After all, the investor wants to make sure his or her investment is being used properly and not "going down the drain" because of bad business decisions. As you can see, by taking money from an investor for an "equity position" in the company, you will have to give up some degree of control.

Sometimes it's better to borrow the money and pay it back with interest because you can completely control the directions the company will take without any interference from people who may know very little about the business but who want to make business decisions in order to protect their investment. Quite often such people may want to move the company opposite to the direction that is best suited to the growth of the company and its long-term goals as you envision them.

At other times, it is better to have an investor "helping" to make the decisions, because it causes your creativity to be balanced by an objective caution that helps protect your working capital. Oftentimes, this gives a better focus to the business. This, in fact, is one of the reasons internal managements often turn to an "outside" board of directors to help guide the management team in making long-term decisions.

Which approach would you rather take?

Return *of* investment and return *on* investment

Every person putting money into a business someone else owns is going to be interested in getting the money back (return of investment) and in how much the money will earn while it is being used (return on investment). After all, if the person put the money in a public company or in a mutual fund that invests in public companies, the person would get (hopefully) a return of the investment together with a "bonus" for the use of the money during a given period of time. Often the "bonus" is the fact that the investment has grown during its tenure and is worth more than when the dollars were originally invested.

If the money is being loaned, the lenders will know just how much interest they will collect before the money is returned. If the money is invested, the investor wants to know the conditions under which the investment will be returned and the method by which the investor can expect a "bonus" for the period of time during which the investment has stayed in the business.

How does the investor's money get returned?

The reason fewer people are interested in "investing" than in "loaning" is there are three methods by which the investment could be returned and the "bonus" earned.

1. If the company is successful in generating profit, it may declare a dividend, in which case each investor will receive an amount of money proportionate to his or her investment.
2. If the company is very successful and is "taken over" or acquired by a larger company, the original investment will probably be worth more than the money actually put into the smaller company. If the acquiring company is already in the public marketplace (that is, its stock is being carried on a public stock exchange), the investor may be able to sell the new stock that was given to him in exchange for his stock in the original company—at a higher dollar value than the money originally invested.
3. If the company is eminently successful in its initial program and decides to accelerate its growth by going into the public marketplace (this is called an initial public offering or IPO), then the stockholders (investors holding equity positions) may get a multiple of dollars for each dollar originally invested. This is not the usual occurrence.

Exit strategy

There are many variations on this theme but it should give you an idea as to how the investor views the investment and what the alternative "exit" strategies may be—that is, how the investor expects to get the original investment and his or her "bonus" out of the company. Sometimes, the investment may be purchased by other parties, either inside or outside the company, if the investor can negotiate this purchase position. This is often done by the second tier or second group of investors when the company has gotten on its feet but needs additional working capital for accelerated growth.

Keep in mind that these methods are for the investor's return *of* investment. If the company is successful, the investor may receive dividends (a share of the distributable profit). This represents the investor's return *on* investment—the "bonus" earned for the use of the investment. Most investors however are sophisticated enough to recognize that even if the business generates an early success it is quite likely that management will use this "profit" to reinvest in the business before they decide to distribute the profits to shareholders (investors). After all, most businesses need to buy inventory, acquire equipment, add personnel, move to larger facilities or make use of the money for any of the many other things that will enable the company to maintain or accelerate its growth—all, by the way, to the ultimate advantage of the investor in the long term.

Getting the money is sometimes the only thing on your mind when the start-up or continuity of your business is at stake. This is a good time, however positive or optimistic you may be about the venture, to get some good professional advice on the downside risks involved—in other words, what will happen and where you (and your family) will be in the event the fruits of your labor and creativity are not realized. An objective perspective will not necessarily deter you from your goals, but it may suggest some alternative directions that may be less problematical or more likely to succeed.

Key points

- Always ensure you have sufficient working capital to achieve your anticipated plateaus according to the time schedule you've designed.

- People will be more inclined to invest or loan if they know you also will have substantial money or assets of your own at risk.

- Be prepared to give up a certain degree of control if you invite others to invest in your business.

- Be aware that the short-term goals of an investor might not be consistent with your long-term goals for the success of the business.

- What additional security are you prepared to put at risk to borrow money?

Worksheet

- What is the difference between a loan to your business and the purchase of an equity position?

- What does amortization mean?

- What kinds of things can be used as security for a loan?

- What is the biggest problem with investors?

- What is the difference between return *of* investment and return *on* investment?

3

The Business Plan: Developing a Road Map

Most business plans are prepared with a single purpose in mind: to generate an interest in the business, which will cause people to either lend money to or invest in the business. There is, however, a much better reason to create such a plan—to give management itself a clear picture of the short-term and long-term goals of the company. A periodic rewriting of the plan will cause you to recognize the shortcomings of the previous plan and adjust your thinking for the future.

Short-term versus long-term goals

In the case of a lemonade stand, the entrepreneur may have the short-term goal of making enough money to buy a bicycle. On the other hand, he or she may have a much greater, long-term goal of growing the business to the point where (a) it can handle additional product lines, such as cookies, sandwiches, and coffee, or (b) it can generate enough activity to open on another street corner (which would entail hiring someone to operate the second location), or even (c) to create a franchise that can be sold to other entrepreneurs because the quality of the product is singular enough in taste to tempt customers away from the competition. Certainly these may be grandiose ideas for the lemonade vendor, but you must understand that long-term goals can only be *achieved* when they've been *conceived*.

Creating the road map to success

To convert a business idea into a business structure, it is important to have a plan that will establish the basic parameters of a successful start-up: design the alternatives to meet the contingencies that will invariably arise (in other words, prepare for the problems and the pitfalls) and create the discipline among the participants to follow the plan. The "business plan," properly prepared, will give you this road map to success. It will examine alternative roads that may prove to be quicker but more dangerous, or slower but with a higher degree of certainty.

You should prepare a plan consistent with the size of your business and the goals it is designed to attain. You have also heard that a business plan has to cover everything. Keep in mind that the larger the plan, the longer the reading, and the less likely it is to be completely read; the purpose is defeated before it has a chance to succeed. Be careful not to use trade or industry language the reader will likely not understand. This will clearly defeat your purpose—whatever it may be—whether to entice personnel to join the company or to intrigue investors to put up their money. Use language anyone can understand, and don't use the excuse that industry jargon is necessary to explain the project. For more information on this issue, see Chapter 9, *Dealing with the Professionals.*

Stick to the basics

The basic business plan should include about 10 fundamental elements. Keep in mind that there is no magic required for its creation. Therefore, there is no given priority schedule necessary in its preparation. Think logically about what the reader may be looking for and design the plan to meet his or her requirements. This may require you to have more than one business plan. Some purposes require a more detailed explanation of certain aspects of the business than others.

1. **Look at the trade or industry of which your business is or will become a part.** Describe its genesis—how it started; how it has developed, and where it is likely to go. This should obviously be designed to show your competitive position in the marketplace.

2. **Describe the company.** Show how your company relates to the entire industry, but more particularly how the idea became (or will become) a reality. Discuss its potential, indicating both the dollars needed as well as the time line required for its growth. Don't forget to indicate why your product or service will be able to take its place in the industry along with—or better yet, in front of—the competition.

3. **Discuss the management.** Management consists of the people, including yourself, who are going to be able to accomplish the short and long-term goals. This will involve disclosure of the education, background, and experience of each person necessary to operate the business. Describe what each person brings to the table that will make his or her participation a factor contributing to the success of the company. Be careful to examine any negative aspect of any

participant before you decide whether or not to include it. It might be better to include prior bankruptcy, for example, and explain it as not being relevant to this business—than to exclude it entirely and be guilty of misrepresentation. Such an omission can lead to an unlimited number of problems later—and substantial liability in many cases. At the very least, it will cause your presentation to fail in terms of accomplishing its designed purpose. See your professional before you make a decision on matters that have such potential negative consequences. Most investors are more concerned about management than any other single element. A discussion of management will show what other people are willing to put at risk, whether it be money, reputation, or both. It gives the investor some comfort in knowing that his or her investment is not the only risk being taken.

4. **Examine the competition.** To better understand why your company will have a competitive edge in the marketplace you need to check out your competitors. If you sell hamburgers, you are clearly in competition with everyone else who sells hamburgers. But, keep in mind, even if you have developed a brand new and unique toy that no one else carries, you are still in competition with everyone else who is selling toys. You will need to understand your competition to properly present your comparative position in the marketplace.

5. **Analyze your target market.** Make sure you can recognize your potential customer. Then discuss the methods by which you expect to reach this customer base. You should include any reference materials that give credibility to your analysis.

6. **Discuss carefully your working capital situation.** You will need to know—and any potential investor will want to know—just how judiciously you will spend your dollars to achieve the different plateaus you expect to reach on the way to your short-term and long-term goals. How long will your present finances last? Will it be enough to satisfy the requirements of the company's strategies?

7. **Discuss future finances.** Future growth will probably require a second round of financial investment. Discuss the purpose of the additional dollars, the goals you intend to attain, and the rationale by which you expect to achieve those goals. The time within which you expect to do these things will be an important element of your analysis.

8. **Look at projections.** Design a format that will show just how much money is required at different stages during the anticipated time line. How many people will you need in six months? How much inventory will you need in the first year? What kind of replacement equipment will be required in the first 24 months? *Be realistic. Investors are not interested in the possible. They are interested in the probable.*

9. **Consider management of operations.** Discuss the job category of each person necessary to operate the business. Will he or she be an employee or will the job be outsourced? Will the products be completely manufactured or merely assembled? Do you need to own real estate or can you rent premises?
10. **Show your investors (or yourself) the payback.** Investors will want to know how you intend to deliver a return on the money invested, and the time parameters during which these payments will be made, as well as the source of the payments. This is often referred to as the "exit strategy"—the method by which the investors can anticipate leaving the business with their original investment intact as well as with any anticipated interest.

Examine the concept in action

Tony, age 11, needed money to buy a bicycle. He decided that going into business was his best opportunity to earn the necessary dollars. He needed to borrow the start-up capital necessary for the business. He developed a business plan and presented it to his father. To be sure, it was a verbal presentation and not a formal written business plan, but the same basic requirements prevailed.

He needed to buy straw baskets, three different kinds of fruit, colored paper to be shredded as "stuffing" for the baskets, ribbon, and plastic wrap. He bought these items, packaged them attractively, and offered them for sale in the neighborhood for Christmas presents. He generated enough money to pay back the loan (his father did not ask for interest), buy his bicycle, give five of his "creations" to members of the family for the holidays, and had enough money left over for two tickets to the ball game.

The following answers were responses to the questions his father asked before committing to the investment in Tony's business.

He went to the market to price his raw materials.
He went to the specialty stores to price other similar products (and to check on the best design and packaging).
He decided how much time he would need to build an appropriate inventory.
He sought advance orders (or at least promises for some advance orders) from some of his potential customers.
He understood the necessity of timing his product properly for the holidays—keeping in mind the shelf life of the product and the time most people would be interested in buying this or an equivalent product.

As you can see, this is not an academic exercise. It is the necessary beginning to any business venture. Selling fruit baskets may be a little simplistic in terms of most businesses, but it contains the basic elements of manufacturing, retailing, and obtaining the capital necessary to start the business. The basics are always the same!

In some cases, the business plan may include advertising materials, charts on the history of the industry, projections on the anticipated growth of the company, and other drawings, concepts, articles, or pictures of that nature.

Following are some elements of a business plan. Although it is not designed to be a complete plan, certain elements are included to give you a "picture" of the business and an idea of how that picture was developed. The primary purpose of the example is to examine a situation where the investment road is a long one and where the investors are told they will not likely see any return of their investment for some time. Note the candor with which this subject is addressed in the sections *Financial outlook and projections* and *Payback or exit strategy for investors*.

BUSINESS PLAN

The following represent certain sections of a business plan. Is the portrayed plan the best possible presentation under the circumstances?

... for the development, manufacture, and distribution of a device designed to conserve fossil fuel by cleaner combustion

... leading to more energy per unit of fuel with lesser cost to the end user

... and less pollution of the environment

History of the problem

The goal of fuel conservation, in all its forms, has been a high priority for many years. Our dependence on fossil fuels for all segments of our economy has even led us to participation in war. This dependence has also prevented us from being independent of many foreign countries, and the future does not appear to suggest significant change.

Air pollution is primarily caused because the fuel does not burn completely. It's the unburned particles that are the problem. The more completely fuel burns, the less pollution—and, of course, the greater the mileage per gallon, or the less fuel being burned. Just think what a 10% reduction in fuel usage would mean to an owner of thousands of trucks, to bus companies, and to the airline industry—to touch only the tip of the proverbial iceberg.

Many alternatives have been and are being developed. These include energy by wind, water, and nuclear power—clearly, long-term solutions to a "now" problem. The concept of fuel conservation has also been addressed, and it is this concept on which our business is predicated.

Personal experience with the concept

A unit has been developed that was tested and sold by me within the past five years. It was successful to the point of providing a 20% fuel savings in a particular test vehicle. (See the attached affidavit.) *Author's Note: Not actually included in this example.*

The negative results of my subsequent marketing effort turned out to be all the reasons why it was imperative that I continue my research. I contacted several owners of large fleets, such as the bus company in Atlanta, operating some 800 busses, plus many other vehicles; the electric company, owning some 6,000 vehicles; trucking companies, and larger and smaller garages for cars, trucks, and buses. The particular device I was selling, I was told, was too heavy and too difficult to install: the fuel line had to be cut, and many people objected to that. In addition, the price was too high, and it was therefore too costly for large fleets to have this device installed.

Succinctly, the problem with the existing unit is threefold:

1. It is inconsistent in its test results with other test vehicles.
2. It is improperly designed for maximum efficiency and minimum cost.
3. Its required attachment technique is time consuming, expensive, and leads to collateral problems that inhibit its purchase.

After extensive examination of the device, I have discovered a method to "handle" the above problems and to make this device acceptable to the consumer at the right price. It is this concept on which this business is predicated.

It is obvious that:

1. The old device was not fully developed and market tested.
2. It was not user friendly.
3. There was no marketing strategy.

4. Fuel catalysts may need to be "tuned" or "adjusted" in accordance with motor design.
5. There were a few changes to the device that would address all of the above.

Method of addressing the problem: The first plateau

Although converters of various types are currently being installed in cars, what about the millions of trucks on the roads, the many buses, the planes in the sky? The adaptation of the design concept is relatively simple, but it is not a feasible business opportunity unless and until it is tested properly under the right circumstances and under the auspices of the appropriate authorities as well for credibility purposes. This is our first level of activity. The device must be tested in a variety of vehicles, in other sources of energy production, and under a variety of conditions to ensure that all questions relative to its viability can be properly answered.

The finished prototype, the application for patent protection, and the manufactured test items will be the first plateau to be reached in the program that follows.

The second plateau: Providing the proof

We will test this device in different parts of the world to gauge its effectiveness with different kinds of fuel, engines, climate, and geography. For these tests, we need a number of prototypes to be installed in average size motor vehicles. As these tests prove successful, as we expect will be the case based on preliminary testing programs, we should be able to initiate the delivery of such devices within a reasonably short period of time.

In a later series of tests, we plan to test a larger device destined for owners of large fleets of motor vehicles (trucking and bus companies) and for the airline industry.

With these devices, we will be able to provide much-needed relief to the producers of motor vehicles as well as the producers of all other fossil fuel–burning machinery—all of whom, I might add, are currently "under the gun" to improve their fuel-burning efficiency in an attempt to stem the pollution problem worldwide.

Since this rather unique device is capable of addressing all areas where fuel is being burned, we find ourselves in a market with virtually no competition and with regulatory requirements strongly in our favor. The potential of the concept could lead us to all kinds of government and commercial "grants" once we establish our credibility in the test market.

There is also no question that the potential financial rewards for providing this service at this crucial time seems almost limitless. The benefits in terms of a potential investor could well be a 20 times return on investment in five years. See the Financial summary. *Author's Note: not included in this example.*

Disclaimer

[*Author's Note*] You will invariably find a paragraph in the prospectus that indicates the conjectural nature of any and all financial projections due to the fact that there is no competitive factor with which you can clearly form a parallel, etc. It is essential that this be included regardless of how definitive you may be due to the conjectural nature of the investment.

Management and outsourcing

Although I am currently the sole person involved in the creation of the company and the only one "on board" conversant with the concept, the appropriate people necessary to create and implement the company and the product are readily available. These people include: (a) engineers to test components and design prototypes and final product; (b) administration, sales, and marketing people who would examine the competitive elements in the marketplace as well as get the product "off the ground" and maximize its sales potential worldwide; (c) legal and accounting people to create the company and look toward the future of investment, patent protection, and investor "exit" strategy.

Although I have had discussions with many of these people to monitor interest and availability, I have been quite circumspect relative to actual disclosure of pertinent elements that need to be protected.

The appropriate people will be brought on board only when it is necessary to do so and within the budgetary constraints of the company.

Because demand for the product will clearly be quite dynamic once the necessary elements have been put into place, the need for immediate production capability dictates that this aspect of the business initially will likely be outsourced. The current concept of business in the general business marketplace also suggests that most administration, sales, and marketing aspects of the business will also likely be outsourced during the early developmental stages of the business.

Finances generally

It is clear, and must be clearly stated, that this project has two substantial financial dynamics:

1. Because I am the sole person on the edge of this potential, the current working capital of the company is not only limited, it is essentially nonexistent.
2. The potential investment return relative to the success of this venture is nothing less than enormous.

Therefore, it is clear that the investor group, at this early stage, should expect to enjoy a substantial position of the equity of the business as a result of their investment being clearly in the nature of a "calculated risk." It is proposed therefore that with the initial capitalization of the initiating company being estimated at approximately $250,000, this aggregate amount shall represent 20% of the stock of the proposed company. This represents the first plateau in terms of investment. It is anticipated that the second plateau will be an investment requirement of $500,000 and will represent approximately 10% of the equity of the company.

Financial outlook and projections

By examining the financial projections (see Exhibit A *[Author's Note: not included in this example]*) it is clear that the *first year* of operations—being involved totally in the experimental and proving stages as well as the production of prototypes for testing purposes—will require expenditures of $100,000 to $150,000 without any possibility of income derived from sales.

The second year, once the concept has been proven, the prototypes produced, and the testing process finished, an additional $50,000 to $100,000 will be needed for selling purposes. At this time sales will have been initiated and an income stream will have been developed.

By the third year, the company will presumably be enjoying the rewards of constant testing. We will be examining the results of our sales in the realistic business community and reworking the existing models to constantly improve the technical and practical elements of the product to ensure a better product at a lower cost, leading to a greater margin of profit.

The fourth year will see us deciding which outsourced aspects of the business could be developed internally for the maximum profit potential in the long term.

Payback or exit strategy for investors

As the developmental aspects of our production suggest collateral designs and devices, the company will likely continue to move in those directions. It is at this time that investors will have an opportunity to invest further in areas that will likely be less problematic in terms of time and development and less conjectural in terms of marketability due to the "piggyback" nature of these new devices based on the success of the original designs.

The possibility of acquisition or public offerings could certainly be explored at that time. With investors' positions on the Board of Directors, these options will be examined from the perspective of both management and the investor.

Do you think this is an honest portrayal? Would any investor be inclined to put money at risk under these circumstances? See Chapter 17, Real People/Success and Failure. *Can you think of any way to paint a more optimistic picture? Would you want to?*

You will note in the section *Management and Outsourcing* that funding for this venture is being sought at a particularly early stage of the business' development. The more normal situation is that a company has already been formed, management is in place and it has already taken its competitive position in the marketplace. In other words, it has a track record to show potential investors exactly how their money will be used to accelerate the growth of the business and, in turn, just how and within what approximate time period their investment either will be returned or will bear fruit.

Although this is the more *unusual* scenario, it is being presented because there are so many people who have ideas and do not have the money to get the project off the ground. This kind of business plan will show you the frustrations involved in making an honest presentation—anything less than which would certainly be foolhardy on the part of the presenter. Deception, misrepresentation, and material omission of fact can lead to serious legal implications—even if the project is a success. Be wary of anyone who suggests such an approach.

On the other hand, would you, as an investor, be inclined to put your money at risk with such a conjectural business future?

Sometimes, the answer to such a dilemma is to take the years of your own time necessary to develop the idea to a point where your presentation can be a little more positive in nature. Which direction would you think is a better alternative? Also keep in mind that the more conjectural the presentation, the higher the percentage of the business and the more control of the business you will likely have to surrender. How would this affect your thinking?

Key points

- Examine your short-term and long-term goals carefully before exposing your business to anyone else.

- Set out the necessary elements in terms of the highest priority first.

- Don't lose sight of the industry parameters and the part in the industry that your business will take.

- Remember that management will be a high priority in terms of what your investors will look at.

- Make sure you define the "exit strategy" for your investors in your business plan.

Worksheet

- What are some of the purposes of a business plan?

- Why is a business plan similar to a road map?

- Name three basics that a business plan should contain.

- What should your business plan say about employees?

- What is the most important thing to most investors?

4

Looking in the Mirror

You may be very creative but not be a whiz with numbers. You may be brilliant at fixing things but not be very careful at keeping tools where they belong. You may be very quick to speak to friends and family but be very uncomfortable when dealing with strangers.

In other words, each of you is better at some things than others. It is important to know what these special talents are. It is even more important, however, to know the things others can do better than you can.

Self-deception

It is time to look in the mirror. Here is where the problem lies with most people. Some people look in the mirror and see not what they are, but what they'd like to be. This is called self-deception, and in business it is especially dangerous. Although it is certainly true that you can develop skills you might not have at any given moment, we are talking, to begin with, about self-realization. It is also true that you can learn the things you don't know, so lack of knowledge at any point in time need not be definitive or critical. But, don't forget the purpose of the exercise: to understand the talent, the experience, the education, the abilities, and the proclivities that you bring to the table. More importantly, recognize the things you don't presently bring to the table so you can make arrangements to have them available when you need them. Any other approach would be contrary to the best interests of your business and its future.

It is, unfortunately, standard procedure in most books to merely tell the reader what it is he or she ought to know. This chapter is devoted to the proposition that the first thing you need to know is who and what you are. No author can give you the answers to that.

Only you can! This chapter, then, is your chapter. Handle it carefully. It will help you set the standards you need to make important life decisions.

(Keep in mind that each question may not pertain to your particular situation. It should, however, keep you ever vigilant on your road.)

∞ ∞

The following questions are personal. They are questions of self-analysis. Some questions might not seem to fit, but they all represent an element of importance. Don't kid yourself. No one will see the answers but you. Be honest; be candid. Then ask yourself: "If someone else answered these questions in this way, what advice would I give them about starting or owning their own business?" What advice would you give yourself based on your score?

1. For those already in the business marketplace:

Yes No

❑ ❑ 3 a. Have you lost your job and can't find another?

❑ ❑ 3 b. Have you been forced to take a position at a lower salary?

❑ ❑ 3 c. Are you in jeopardy of losing your job?

❑ ❑ 2 d. Is your job subject to replacement by equipment or computers?

❑ ❑ 3 e. Are your family needs increasing while your income remains the same?

❑ ❑ 3 f. Have you been forced to liquidate hard assets to maintain your standard of living?

❑ ❑ 3 g. Can you see your remaining cash and assets eroding as time goes on?

❑ ❑ 3 h. Are you at an age where finding a new job is difficult because younger people are just as well schooled or just as experienced as you?

❑ ❑ 3 i. Are you in jeopardy of losing your health insurance?

❑ ❑ 3 j. Have you failed to establish any kind of retirement plan?

❑ ❑ 3 k. Are you just plain tired of taking orders?

❑ ❑ 6 l. Is your job so stressful that it is affecting your health?

❑	❑	4	m.	Do you feel it's almost too late to change the course of your life?
❑	❑	5	n.	Have you and your spouse been thinking about this for a long time?
❑	❑	2	o.	Do you have a new freedom because the children are now on their own?

If your "Yes" answers add up to 20 points or more, it's time to consider a change.

❧

2. For those not yet in the business marketplace:

Yes   No

❑	❑	3	a.	Have you been harboring a special dream for a business venture?
❑	❑	4	b.	Do you think you've got talents that are being wasted?
❑	❑	2	c.	Have you run across an interesting business concept lately?
❑	❑	3	d.	Has somebody come to you with a good idea for a partnership?
❑	❑	5	e.	Do you have a particular expertise that could become the framework for a business?
❑	❑	5	f.	Do you have a hobby that can be turned into a profitable business enterprise?
❑	❑	4	g.	Do you want to learn about a whole new field?
❑	❑	2	h.	Do you want to move from your present community?
❑	❑	3	i.	Have you seen a business or a profit margin that got you excited?
❑	❑	2	j.	Are you technically oriented?
❑	❑	2	k.	Are you sales oriented?
❑	❑	2	l.	Are you financially oriented?
❑	❑	2	m.	Are you mechanically oriented?

If your "Yes" answers add up to 20 points or more, you may be ready to look for a new adventure.

❦

3. For everyone, from a personal perspective:

How well do you know yourself?

Yes	No			
❑	❑	4	a.	Are you able to maintain objectivity about a business idea?
❑	❑	4	b.	Are you able to candidly discuss your own abilities and inadequacies with others?
❑	❑	4	c.	Are you able to take advice from professionals?
❑	❑	4	d.	Do you know people on whose opinions you can rely?
❑	❑	4	e.	Do you understand the basics of operating a business?
❑	❑	4	f.	Do you understand the basic differences between a profit and loss statement, a cash flow analysis, and a balance sheet?
❑	❑	4	g.	Do you understand the basic language of a lease and a contract?
❑	❑	4	h.	Do you know what a franchise is all about?
❑	❑	4	i.	Are you a gambler?
❑	❑	3	j.	Are you prepared to make compromises?
❑	❑	5	k.	Are you willing to give up some short-term goals for a long-term success?
❑	❑	5	l.	Is your family willing to sacrifice in the short term for a long-term success?
❑	❑	6	m.	Is your spouse in sync with your goals and aspirations?

If your "Yes" answers add up to 23 points or more, you may be prepared to examine an alternative future.

❦

4. For everyone, from a very personal perspective:

Is your ego a delicate thing?

Yes	No			
❑	❑	3	a.	Are you able to accept criticism from others?
❑	❑	3	b.	Are you capable of delegating responsibility?
❑	❑	3	c.	Can you live with the mistakes of others?
❑	❑	4	d.	Are you willing to accept responsibility for your mistakes?

Yes	No			
❏	❏	4	e.	Do you get along with your peers in the workplace?
❏	❏	4	f.	Do you get along with your superiors in the workplace?
❏	❏	5	g.	Do you get along with your subordinates in the workplace?
❏	❏	4	h.	Is your marriage strong enough to sustain some frustrating times?
❏	❏	4	i.	Are you willing to accept menial tasks like sweeping the floor or washing the dishes?
❏	❏	4	j.	Are you willing to get your hands dirty?
❏	❏	4	k.	Have you ever served in the military?

If your "Yes" answers add up to 25 points or more, you can probably handle most aspects of entrepreneurship.

ೲ∽ೲ

5. **For everyone, from a business perspective:**

Have you examined the marketplace?

Yes	No			
❏	❏	4	a.	Have you ever done any research work in business or in school?
❏	❏	4	b.	Have you ever subscribed to trade journals in your trade or industry?
❏	❏	4	c.	Do you know how to do a comparative analysis?
❏	❏	2	d.	Have you ever read a disclosure document for the purpose of purchasing corporate shares or a franchise?
❏	❏	4	e.	Have you ever dealt with a lawyer, an accountant, a business broker, a banker, or a business consultant?
❏	❏	3	f.	Have you ever done a marketing survey?
❏	❏	3	g.	Have you ever prepared a business plan?
❏	❏	3	h.	Have you ever filled out a résumé or a job application?
❏	❏	3	i.	Have you ever applied for a job?
❏	❏	3	j.	Have you ever applied for a loan?

If your "Yes" answers add up to 15 points or more, you've got a good start on examining a new future.

∽∾

6. Available personal finances:

How much money do you have available for investment? The answer to this question depends on the following:

a. How much money do you have in liquid assets? Cash?

b. How much money do you need for personal or family maintenance while you are waiting until you can depend on the profits from the business?

c. How much money do you need for working capital if your initial break-even time period does not prove to be accurate?

d. How quickly can your other assets be converted to cash?

e. How much of a penalty will you have to pay for the privilege of this conversion?

f. What effect will this conversion have on your short- and long-term goals?

This requires a simple "life equation" that must be carefully analyzed with some reasonable objectivity. Think about discussing this with a professional financial advisor.

∽∾

7. Experiential financial obligations:

Have you ever made a monthly payment on an obligation?

Yes	No			
❏	❏	3	a.	Have you ever paid a home mortgage?
❏	❏	4	b.	Have you ever paid for a car on a time payment plan?
❏	❏	5	c.	Have you ever bought major household appliances on a time payment plan?
❏	❏	3	d.	Have you found it possible to fit such a payment schedule into your monthly budget?
❏	❏	4	e.	Are you prepared to take on the responsibility for this kind of monthly program?

If your "Yes" answers add up to 8 points or more, you understand one of the most important elements of owning and operating your own business.

ထာထာ

8. **Examining your priorities:**

Are you prepared to put your business activity on your highest priority level?

Yes   No

❑   ❑   5   a. Have you discussed this with your spouse?

❑   ❑   5   b. Have you discussed this with your children?

❑   ❑   5   c. Are you prepared to subordinate the emotional needs of your family to that of your business on those occasions when the business demands your time and energy?

Your "Yes" answers need to add up to 15 points if you have children. Your "Yes" answers need to add up to 10 points if you don't have children.

ထာထာ

9. **Learning and delegating:**

Are you prepared to accept responsibility for aspects of business about which you have either limited or no knowledge or experience?

Yes   No

❑   ❑   5   a. Are you prepared to spend the time to learn how to do these things, or at least learn enough about them to supervise others?

❑   ❑   5   b. Are you prepared to leave the responsibility to others for those things you are incapable of doing or ill-prepared to handle?

Your "Yes" answers need to add up to 10 points for you to feel comfortable going forward in a new adventure.

ထာထာ

10. **"Running over the hot coals":**

Have you completely and objectively examined your background, experience, and inclinations with respect to this new business venture? Are you excited (E) or disappointed (D) at the thought of:

E or D a. Dealing with retail customers?

E or D b. Handling bookkeeping and basic accounting procedures?

E or D c. Maintaining inventory and an appropriate ordering system?

E or D d. Creating advertising concepts and campaigns?

E or D e. Studying a new industry?

E or D f. Dealing with employees and employee problems?

E or D g. Handling cash at a counter?

E or D h. Maintaining strict hygiene discipline?

E or D i. Doing outside sales calls?

E or D j. Doing cold calls?

E or D k. Doing telephone solicitations

You need more E's than D's to understand the focus necessary to be an entrepreneur.

☙❧

11. **Examining the harsh realities of ownership:**

   Are you looking at a business because it looks like fun or because it looks like it would make a lot of money?

   Yes No

   ❏ ❏ a. Can you afford to buy a business and treat it like a hobby?

   ❏ ❏ b. Can you afford to buy a business that generates less money than you or your family need to live?

   ❏ ❏ c. Do you have either an auxiliary income or a deep reservoir of savings in case the business generates less money than anticipated?

   ❏ ❏ d. Are you sure you have done enough homework to ensure the dollars you see are the dollars you'll get?

   You need 3 or more "Yes" answers here to have a realistic perspective on the problems of owning your own business.

☙❧

12. **Analyzing the practical aspects of your new environment:**

   If you are moving to a new community or a new climate, have you considered the following?

   Yes No

   ❏ ❏ a. Have you examined what all four seasons are like?

   ❏ ❏ b. Have you looked for a church or social group with which you will have something in common?

  ☐   ☐   c. Have you examined the price of housing (rental or purchase) and determined you can afford it?

  ☐   ☐   d. Have you examined the school system to ensure it satisfies the needs of the family and its growth potential?

You need to answer all four questions with "Yes." If you can't, you're not ready to move.

∞∞

13. Your knowledge of the business:

Have you examined the industry you are entering?

Yes No

  ☐   ☐   a. Does the industry have a future?

  ☐   ☐   b. Does your industry (and your business) maintain state-of-the-art products and services?

  ☐   ☐   c. Are you sure the marketplace is not saturated?

  ☐   ☐   d. Have you asked a person who owns one?

  ☐   ☐   e. Do you know the level of responsibility you will be taking on?

  ☐   ☐   f. Are you totally prepared for the realities of the business?

  ☐   ☐   g. Are you aware of the aggravations and the frustrations of the business?

You need to answer all seven questions with a "Yes." Or, do more homework!

∞∞

14. A real comparative analysis:

Have you examined your personal finances to be sure of the following?

Yes No

  ☐   ☐   a. Do you have enough money to keep the business going if it brings in less cash (or even a great deal less cash) than you anticipated?

  ☐   ☐   b. Do you have a reservoir of dollars that you can draw upon if the business continues to be disappointing for an extended period of time?

  ☐   ☐   c. Will these dollars (to help the business survive) be taken away from the needs of your personal living expenses?

❏ ❏ d. Have you analyzed just how much money you will need to properly support the family during the early—and possibly nonprofit—period, of the business?

❏ ❏ e. Have you discussed this with other responsible family members?

❏ ❏ f. Have you anticipated some of the extraordinary expenses the family may need to accommodate during the early days of your new business activity?

❏ ❏ g. Do you realize you can see a clearer picture of the cash flow and profit of a business that is already in existence than you can conjecture about a business that has not yet opened?

❏ ❏ h. Do you need this comfort zone in order to properly function in your new role as an entrepreneur?

❏ ❏ i. Have you ever been in the position of entrepreneur before this venture?

❏ ❏ j. Have you spoken to others who have had the experience of this kind of venture?

❏ ❏ k. Do you feel you have as much ability and confidence in your ability as they have?

If you are contemplating the purchase of a franchise...

❏ ❏ l. Have you asked the franchisor about these subjects?

❏ ❏ m. Have you asked other franchisees about these subjects?

If you have more than 3 "No's" to these questions, you should do a reappraisal of your finances, or do more homework.

∞∞

15. **Examining what competition is all about:**

Do you understand the nature of the competition in your business?

Yes No

❏ ❏ a. Have you ever been in a competitive situation before, even in the corporate world?

❏ ❏ b. Were you able to cope with the disappointment of losing to a competitor?

❏ ❏ c. Were you able to bounce back and continue to function after such a disappointment?

❑ ❑ d. Were you able to objectively analyze the reason for having lost to your competitor?

❑ ❑ e. Were you able to correct the elements that were noted as the cause of the loss?

❑ ❑ f. Do you have the ability to learn from your mistakes?

❑ ❑ g. Do you have the ability to absorb and utilize that learning for a more effective "next time?"

❑ ❑ h. Do you understand the nature of "healthy competition?"

❑ ❑ i. Do you believe that competition can be to your advantage?

❑ ❑ j. Have you found it comfortable to spend time, on a business level, with your competition?

❑ ❑ k. Have you found it uncomfortable to spend time, on a personal level, with your competition?

❑ ❑ l. Have you ever tried to work out a mutually advantageous arrangement with your competition?

❑ ❑ m. Do you think such an arrangement can be helpful in the right circumstances?

If you are contemplating the purchase of a franchise...

❑ ❑ n. Have you asked the franchisor about these subjects?

❑ ❑ o. Have you asked other franchisees about these subjects?

If you have more than 3 "No's," you should devote some time to the study of competition in the marketplace.

∞∞

16. You and your family:

What kind of an entrepreneur are you?

Yes No

❑ ❑ a. Are you interested in taking a risk for a high reward?

❑ ❑ b. Are you more interested in getting a good day's pay for an honest day's labor?

❑ ❑ c. If you have taken the conservative road before, has this been a satisfactory one for your family?

❑ ❑ d. If you were to choose to be less conservative in the future, would your financial portfolio really allow you to take that road?

❑ ❑ e. Would your family be able to maintain their style of living in the event the road turned out to be a rough one?

❑ ❑ f. Is the family willing to make such an adjustment?

❑ ❑ g. Have you candidly examined this alternative with the other members of your family?

If you answered "No" to more than 1 question, you may want to revisit your thinking about becoming an entrepreneur.

❦

17. Some specific business questions about leases:

Do you understand the reasons for having a particular kind of location in the trade or industry you are entering?

Yes No

❑ ❑ a. Have you done a competitive analysis of the location?

❑ ❑ b. Have you done any market research on the location in terms of your customer base?

❑ ❑ c. Have you examined the municipal records to ensure there will be no building or demolition in your immediate neighborhood?

❑ ❑ d. Have you examined your lease to ensure there will be no surprises in the future?

❑ ❑ e. Have you sought the advice of a professional with regard to all aspects of your lease?

If you are considering the purchase of a franchise...

❑ ❑ f. Have you asked the franchisor about these subjects?

❑ ❑ g. Have you asked other franchisees about these subjects?

You must answer all these questions in the affirmative. If you can't, you are not ready to sign a lease.

❦

18. Some additional business questions:

On whose information have you relied to make your final judgment?

Yes No

❑ ❑ a. If you are considering a franchise, have you sought information from sources other than the franchisor?

❏ ❏ b. Have you sought the advice of professionals in each field that is appropriate: an accountant for financial; a lawyer for legal; a marketing person for the marketplace?

❏ ❏ c. Have you sought information from competitors and vendors in the same business?

❏ ❏ d. Have you sought information from independents as well as franchisees of other franchises in the same trade or industry?

❏ ❏ e. Have you examined and compared "the numbers" with any vendors in the industry?

❏ ❏ f. Have you inquired of vendors about state-of-the-art equipment and supplies?

❏ ❏ g. Have you read any trade journals about the business you are about to enter?

❏ ❏ h. Have you done an analysis of the future of the industry?

❏ ❏ i. Are you satisfied that your personality and experience are compatible with the requirements of the business you are examining?

❏ ❏ j. Have you examined other businesses to ensure you are taking the best advantage of your personal and business assets?

If you can't say "Yes" to most of these questions, you are not yet ready to take on the responsibilities of a new business.

◌◌◌

The above questions represent the beginning of your personal exercise. No single section is definitive. Don't be afraid to seek professional advice. The few dollars spent early on will save many dollars and a multitude of disappointments later in the game. Whatever you do, be honest with yourself!

5

How Do I Choose "My" Business?

One part of the equation of success is learning how to handle business basics. Another part is deciding just what business you want to handle. Some people suggest you do the things you enjoy most. Others advise you to stick to the things you do best. The fact is there is no single piece of advice that can stand alone as the secret to embarking on a successful business adventure. The secret, if there is any, is in making an honest assessment of both your inclination and your expertise.

Looking in the mirror

When you look at yourself in your "self-assessment" mirror, be very careful you don't see merely what you want to see; you must recognize what is really there. See Chapter 4, *Looking in the Mirror*. Self deception can be your first step to disaster. Honesty is the best policy, especially when you're dealing with yourself. No one else will ever know, but you will!

When you are examining your mirror image, be careful to include all your personal experience, your education, and your workplace knowledge. Be even more careful to recognize those things you don't find in your background. This is the only way to ensure the availability of those talents, those workplace tools, that are so necessary for the creation, maintenance, and success of your business.

Opening up your book of choices

One of the biggest difficulties is deciding which of your talents or inclinations is a hobby (avocation) and which is convertible to a business venture (vocation). Some can be both, and some, unfortunately, cannot be either. You may be proficient at the piano, the harmonica, or the guitar. Your level of proficiency, however great, may still not be appropriate in the competitive marketplace. On the other hand, merely listening to music, and liking it, may put you in a position to study music or take additional schooling in music that could lead to an involvement in a music company in a variety of different positions. Don't discard your talent as a possible vocation merely because it appears problematical at first glance or because you recognize your talent is something less than deserving of a Pulitzer Prize or an Academy Award.

Keep an open mind

Sometimes it helps to find the right business by the process of elimination. If you're "all thumbs" in the woodworking shop, it might suggest this is not the most logical direction to take for a business. On the other hand, if you've always been good at building models, you might carry this talent over forward to construction, engineering, drafting or architecture—maybe even dentistry. You must open your mind and reach for the kind of opportunity that can utilize your skill or your talent.

Clearly, being a basketball enthusiast should not lead you to think you should try out for the NBA. It takes more than a modicum of talent to be on the team. However, the enjoyment of the sport can lead to many directions in the sporting world when combined with other talents. If you are good at photography or writing, your enthusiasm for sports could take you in a variety of directions, such as magazines, newspapers, radio, or T.V.

One of the problems in today's society is that some people, being especially proficient at a particular thing, end up doing it. And some of them end up being terribly unhappy about having chosen it as their primary source of income.

The Pete Leggett Story

Pete Leggett was getting ready for retirement after 40 years at the same job. He was an engineer, and his specialty, his "chosen" field, had allowed him to keep the same job since he joined the company.

At a recent gathering of friends, he was paid a compliment by an old school chum. "You know, Pete, it's great to see someone get to the end of the road after 40 years, especially after holding a great job all that time." Pete's answer was shocking to his friend. "I appreciate the thought," Pete replied, "but I have to tell you that the last 10 years on the job were the most boring and unsatisfying of my life."

The question this leaves us with is, What is your real goal? Make sure you've picked the right one. This is one reason why today's marketplace is made up of so many people who are in their second or third business venture or vocation. Be careful not to make that mistake. Tony (see Chapter 3, *The Business Plan),* for example, did not go into the fruit basket business as a life's work. But he is currently in the marketing department of a big company. How can you relate these examples to your talents and your business dreams?

The ultimate purpose

Many times, after starting a college career, a student will change his or her course of study. She may start off with the intention of becoming an engineer and then decide, halfway through this course of study, that she'd really like to be a veterinarian. He may be studying architecture and later decide he'd rather be the owner of a small business. This is what college is designed to do. It is to help you structure your ultimate purpose.

What is exciting when you're 18 might not be so exciting when you're 22. Even more important, what is exciting at 22 might not be exciting when you're 45. Is it too late to change? In today's society and in today's business marketplace, "change" seems to be as much the rule as "consistency." It is this prerogative to change your mind that keeps the life program exciting.

Inclination is the first order of business

Certainly, if you don't like rodents, you would not go into rodent control. If you don't like heights, you would not go into roof repair. If you don't like blood, you would not elect to become a surgeon or a paramedic.

What about profit?

When thinking about business, whether you are considering a job as an employee or a business venture as an entrepreneur, you must address the question of personal income, or profit. Although it is theoretically possible to operate on a "break-even" basis, that is, not having either a profit or a loss, the more likely scenario is that you will operate with one or the other, a profit or a loss. If you are operating a "charitable" venture (and can afford to subsidize it with your own money), then operating at a loss can be acceptable. Your profit will be in "good works" as opposed to dollars. Aside from the charitable venture, however, profit is a mandatory consideration because it is the only way to maintain the continuity of a business.

Consider the case of Patsy Chale. Patsy operated a successful retail business as well as a religious bookstore. Not only was the bookstore unprofitable, it was becoming a drain on the successful retail business. After a while, it became clear (to the uninvolved observer) that maintaining the bookstore could seriously jeopardize the operation of the retail business. Patsy had to make a very difficult judgment based on a dynamic alternative. She closed the bookstore and devoted her energies to the retail business. Hopefully, Patsy will see the day when the retail business is strong enough to, once again, subsidize the good works that were so important to her and to her church. It was quite clear that Patsy's failure to close the bookstore in timely fashion could have jeopardized her entire business complex—including the bookstore.

Therefore, as you consider your inclination and your talents, you must also consider the element of profit and you must decide just how important the dollar value is to your thinking.

Fun or profit...but beware the caution

There are many people who would rather be in a business they enjoy with smaller profit than at a job or in a business they don't enjoy with a larger profit.

There is a caution here, however. In some cases, changing professions or industries because a job is not satisfying is not necessarily the answer. Remember that the grass often appears greener on the other side of the fence. Yet, very often, cutting the grass may be a better answer than crossing the fence. You may be able to effect changes in your job description or in the way you perform your job. You may be able to use different equipment or different techniques that will dramatically change your outlook. It is a wise man or woman who examines these alternatives before merely "jumping ship."

The grass may not be greener on the other side, and by making too many career changes you can get the reputation of being something less than stable. Although you certainly should not hesitate to change if you feel strongly about it, it is always best to analyze the alternatives as objectively as possible before you make such a decision. Be careful when you make this decision because it is important. It will become a part of your personality as well as a part of your involvement with other people and with your family.

Another interesting story is that of Carl, who had a marvelous talent for the piano. Today Carl is a professional piano player who has certainly earned the respect of his peers and his audiences. Unfortunately, Carl's income is much smaller than he would like. This has led to a terrible frustration. Even with his piano tuning and teaching thrown in for additional income, Carl's frustration is quite strong. What would you suggest Carl consider?

How would you resolve a similar problem in your own life? Would it help if you were in a business that had a salable equity involved?

"By the seat of his pants"—or otherwise

Although it is appropriate to start from the beginning and examine concepts like the lemonade stand, the fruit basket, and the wooden deer, you must be prepared to face the reality of business in a complex business marketplace.

Years ago, airplane pilots used to fly "by the seat of their pants." The expression derives from the fact that the pilot could pretty much tell what the aspects of the plane were by merely observing the wings, the ground, etc. In today's aircraft, the pilot must be able to read, analyze, and understand a whole variety of complex equipment to properly handle an aircraft that holds not 3 people, but 300 people.

The business equivalent is not much different. Years ago, people would kind of "muddle through" the exercise of starting and maintaining a business. Part of the reason those people enjoyed some degree of success was that as business intruded into suburban areas, where each business was unique, competition was not a dynamic factor. Another reason was that the tax consequences of business profit as well as environmental and legal requirements were a good deal less complicated.

Today, to say the least, the marketplace is different. For those of you who have already been in the business sector, the word "competition" has certainly become a significant part of your vocabulary. For those of you who are entering the business world for the first time, you may be sure that "competition" will always be a part of your thinking, your planning, and your future. It is not necessarily something to be afraid of; it is merely another element of your business activity that you must factor into your equation.

So far as taxes are concerned, you should be aware that between payroll taxes, sales taxes, and income taxes, every aspect of your business, from the time you start to the time you sell your business, will be affected by the tax implications of state, federal, and local government.

It is for this reason that the proper study of "business" is not just understanding the trade or industry of which your business will be a part. It is understanding the nature of business—from financial to marketing, from retail to wholesale, from investment to profit, from margins to markups, from partnerships to corporations, from leases to contracts.

Those few things might give you an idea that education is the beginning of the game. Perhaps the most significant education factor of all is that good businesspeople know that learning is a day-to-day activity to which there is no definitive end. Every day that you learn something about business in general or your business in particular is a day that you get better at what you do and closer to the goals in your business that represent success.

As you examine your inclinations and your choices, you must also factor in the business knowledge and experience you bring with you—as well as those things you are unable to bring to the table. Be sure you examine the questions available in Chapter 4, *Looking in the Mirror.*

Key points

- Making an honest self-assessment should be your first order of business.
- Decide what you enjoy the most, but don't allow it to become the sole aspect of your thinking.
- Keep in mind that every field of interest has many business opportunities available as a part of it.
- Always recognize the many aspects of competition in your business field.
- Be aware of the tax implications of your business at all stages of development.

Worksheet

- What is the difference between a vocation and an avocation?
- How can you help make a choice of business based on the process of elimination?
- Why is profit a significant factor to consider in the choice of your business?
- Why is the business marketplace so different today than it was a generation ago?
- What kinds of taxes will you have to be responsible for in your business?

6

Basic Business Principles

This chapter is designed to help you understand the differences between effective and ineffective business procedures, and to give you a format for the future. It does not contain any great secrets. It is merely a reflection of those human elements that have proven to be successful in the current marketplace—and those that have not. It is a toolbox from which you can take whichever item you find most appropriate to serve your particular business and personal needs.

Survive and prosper

You will find that doing business in the "new marketplace" is not going to merely involve computer technology. It will require an entirely different attitude! Previously, management had a certain loyalty to employees, and the employees had a certain loyalty to management. They stayed with the company, often at the expense of moving to a warmer climate or a more hospitable environment. The company, on the other hand, took care of the employees' health program. This was a real benefit to the employees, with a commensurate but acceptable cost factor to the company. It was a concept of American life in the American marketplace.

In today's urban society, with crime in the streets and all the problems that go with high traffic and smog-filled air, employees are constantly looking for a less complex lifestyle in an environment where children will be safer and less prone to involvement with the criminal element. Their loyalty to the company is strained. Companies are finding they have to look for a competitive edge in a different way. "Downsizing" has become a byword, and cutting back on fringe benefits like health insurance for employees has become the rule rather than the exception. Attitudes are different! The profit motive—

the "bottom line"—has become the highest priority in business. The concept of American life in the American business marketplace has changed.

It is a time when the win-win concept is failing. It is much more a philosophy of adjusting your expectations. It is not so much a question of how much you can win as it is a question of how much you have to give up to survive. In this context, you must think of negotiating instead of mandating. You must think of understanding what the other side needs instead of insisting on your goals no matter what. You must think of combining efforts instead of fighting the system. If you can do this, you can survive and prosper.

Curing the failure syndrome:
Failure is not the end of the road

It is always easier to put the blame for failure on someone other than yourself. It is instinctive to reach out for a scapegoat. The "mea culpa" approach is usually saved for Sundays. During the work week, it's a matter of finding out who made the mistake. The problem is that this attitude usually slows down the curing process. You think every failure must be cured before you can move on. *Remember that failure is not the end of the road. It is merely a stop on the journey. The idea is to make it a short stop—and then go on.* To get back on the road, back in the race, you must recognize the failure, find the failed principle on which it is based, fix it, and go on! Forget who did it even if you really think someone else was responsible. You cannot afford to allow self-pity or any other form of self-indulgence to move you away from the goal. Fix it and move on. If you don't, secondary problems will invariably result.

Success is the flip side of failure

Failure is merely the malfunction of an idea or implementation of an idea. The other side of the coin is the proper function of the idea or implementation: success. No one is immune to failure. The difference is that some people recover more quickly than others. The ones that do recover quickly usually talk about their failure because they consider it a stepping stone to a subsequent success. The ones who don't recover so easily never tell you anything. One of the problems is that some people almost seem to prefer failure as a goal. They are afraid to succeed because success creates new responsibilities. After all, as a failure, less will be expected of you than if you are successful. Getting used to failure is easier. People's expectations of you and your ability decrease each time. There will be less pressure on you each time. Eventually, they will expect nothing from you—and you're off the hook. This may seem like a very negative perspective, but there are people who adopt this thinking. Don't let it happen to you!

You cannot let failure invade and pervade all other things. It can become like a cancer and infect everything else you do. Stop the effects of failure. Do your analysis and move on. Remember what success is: it is the fulfillment of your own expectations.

The problem of unrealistic expectations

Some setbacks can be brought on by unrealistic expectations. When you fall short of total fulfillment, you're going to feel disappointment, depression, and anger. Be careful not to get stuck in the "mourning" period, or you may develop a failure mentality. To start with, make sure the goals are within the capabilities of your organization or your team. Too many failures will inevitably cause you to develop a failure mentality. You must recognize your areas of vulnerability, and the areas of potential failure, and avoid them.

When you can't avoid them, view your failures as a stepping stone. Do some self-analysis. Why did you fail? What can you learn from the setback? Failure often liberates you to take risks that can lead to success. Adjust your expectations and keep the goals simple and within the grasp of your competence.

The role of discipline

To readjust the equilibrium of the business, you will be tempted to discover whose responsibility it was to get the job done. Once this is established, you will probably think it's appropriate or even necessary to decide the discipline required to prevent such a mistake from happening again. The discipline will invariably create a glitch in the team effort so necessary for the business to maintain and succeed. What will the blame and the discipline ultimately accomplish? Probably more of a negative than a positive to the continuity and success of the business. You've accomplished the wrong goal. It's very much like winning the battle and losing the war. Don't even be tempted. The attitude of the "new marketplace" is to get the job done. Success breeds success. Blame and discipline lead to fear. Fear can be a short-term incentive, but it will never stand the test of time.

Bonus to the best

If anything, consider using the failure as a method to motivate the team. Use the failure as a basis for establishing short- and long-term goals. In other words, use the failure as a stepping stone. Get the team to work smarter by giving them a reason to succeed. Sometimes a "dollar reason" will help get the job done better and more quickly. The dollars, from a management standpoint, will likely turn out to be a positive investment rather than a negative expense. Most times these dollars will motivate the employees to preserve inventory or eliminate wasted time. Invariably, it will lead to greater profits. And the team will recognize that blame is not going to be a part of your thinking. They will know that success is the bottom line, and they will contribute because they will want to be among the winners.

Sharing the problem

The best ideas usually come from conferring about what caused the glitch in the first place. In the advertising business, there is a saying that at a conference about ideas you should put everything on the table. Nothing is silly, outrageous, or ridiculous unless the group agrees that it is. You can't shoot down your own idea without presenting it to the group. This means that you have to put your ego at risk and take a chance at looking the fool if the group thinks the idea is lousy. But that's the way it should be. An idea should not be credited just to the person who created it anyway. The people who deserve equal credit are those who took it from its birth to maturity, the people who gave it body and made it fit, made it work to get the job done. Sharing the problem is the best way to get the collective minds in sync to put flesh on the skeleton of an idea and make it function.

Memo me to death

Sitting in a corner office and being the conduit through which filter all the memoranda in a company usually means that you are getting the idea late. It is no longer fresh in the mind of the creator. Time will be needed to establish a conference with those others who might be able to contribute to its growth. And the competition, by this time, has readied its new product or its new advertising message for the streets. One executive noted that on a good day, it was likely "my vice presidents would memo me to death." Moving quickly is going to be another method of the new business marketplace. That's what things like e-mail are all about. Don't continue to dance around the May Pole until the idea becomes stale or the creator of the idea is working for a different company. Get together now and see if the idea makes any sense. If it does, do it! Now!

People look for excuses for their failures: And remember, excuses abound!
My marketplace is saturated with competition

Competition is the natural outgrowth of success in the marketplace. As a successful competitor, you must be prepared to maintain your position in the marketplace by working harder and smarter all the time. Those who think their initial momentum will carry the day without further investment of time, creativity, and energy will be the losers. Competition should motivate you to speed up, not to slow down.

We can't handle the work

The ability to handle the work on a profitable level requires you to assess your team, your equipment, and your other resources to ensure you are maximizing their effectiveness in a competitive environment.

My franchisor makes it impossible to survive

A franchise contract is normally inviolate. If the franchisor is performing under the terms and conditions of the contract, you are obliged to perform as well. Only the authorized items and services may be offered; paying the royalty on time is an absolute requirement. The obligations will not go away. Take a positive attitude. Make the relationship work! Take advantage of the services offered by your franchisor.

My customers demand too much

Customers' demands are the keys to the game. They can ask for value for their money and they are entitled to receive it. If you can't service and satisfy your customer base, it is time to reevaluate your desire and your ability to stay in the business.

I've exhausted my growth potential

It is time to reexamine the spectrum of activities (products and services) you offer to your customer base. Should it be expanded? Time to examine your customers. Are there ways to increase your customer base? Are there ways to increase the amount of purchases per customer? Is there a better delivery system? Is there a way you can gain a competitive edge?

My people can't handle their responsibilities

It is time to examine your people. Do you need more or fewer? Do you have to change the caliber or level of expertise? Will training help to win the day? Each employee has a role to play and should be properly integrated into the business family.

Take a look at the difference that an "employee relationship" can have even at a time when the owner wants to sell the business.

Katie and Roger

Two small business dynasties were in trouble. Katie had ten retail locations but had remained quite aloof from her store managers. As the operational problems multiplied and as she became less enamored of the business, Katie decided to move on. Unfortunately, Katie failed to act quickly enough to stop the proverbial snowball from picking up speed until it was too late to salvage the business. The ultimate result was closure of many of the stores—some, after the managers became disenchanted and left. Others were closed before giving the managers an opportunity to exercise their own judgment in a business their experience might have helped to improve or at least maintain. Katie had no confidence in their business judgment, probably because she really didn't know much about their thinking, their personalities, their goals, or even their anticipated involvement in the future of their respective operations.

Roger, on the other hand, also had ten retail locations in a very similar geography with relatively the same growth potential. Immediately after acquiring the business operation, Roger made a concentrated effort to create a close working relationship with each of his ten managers, as well as with all the operational people of the company—literally, from the manager of his central plant facility to the young delivery boy. It was his habit to take each manager to lunch once a month. Sometimes he would discuss the business of the shop; sometimes he would examine and discuss current problems faced by the industry. Other times he would avoid discussing business completely; it would be a personal lunch.

Roger created this same personal relationship with the rest of his employees as well. When the business as a whole started to get bigger than Roger's ability to cope, Roger called on all of his people—one at a time. He candidly discussed his inability to maintain the business' integrity over the long term and gave each of his people an opportunity to consider purchasing a shop before he placed the shops on the open market for sale. What happened is one answer to the question of the employer-employee relationship.

Two of the ten shops were sold to the manager of the central plant facility. Two more were sold to his controller. Two managers were anxious to become owners but couldn't find the necessary capital. Because of their relationship, however, both managers agreed to stay, making it easier for Roger to find a buyer who was unfamiliar with the industry but who recognized the potential of the industry—and the individual locations. Two more shops were sold to friends of "insiders." The balance of four shops were sold to strangers. It should be noted that even those sales were expedited by the positive attitude of all Roger's employees, who were quick to speak of the personal and honest relationship he had maintained with each of them during his tenure.

Your relationship with your employees can never be understated. It can be a key to the continuity and success of your business.

I didn't have the time to do it right

Time is an interesting part of everything we do. Note how we talk about time: we use it; we lose it; we can't find it but we can make more of it, and, more often than not, it is not on our side. Time constantly escapes us, but it can also be recaptured. Experience, in fact, tells us quite a bit about "time." The best labor-saving device is "do it tomorrow." The fastest road to success is "do it now." One of the worst expressions relative to time is "do it later."

A difference in priorities

Procrastination is often a very subtle cause of failure, and the interesting thing is that procrastination may actually amount to no more than a difference in priorities. Take a look at some of the results.

a. Don't put off a job on which other activities depend. You can't put on a roof until you have the house built and you can't build the house unless you have a foundation.
b. Be sure of your personal priorities. If your real priority is to have a good time, then stop kidding yourself about attaining career goals or any other goals. Be honest with yourself. Give up your unrealistic fantasies of achievement. Live with the consequences of your pleasure priorities. Be real!
c. Overcoming procrastination does not mean taking in an overwhelming amount of work or a specific job to be done within an unrealistic time frame. Don't allow a buildup to reach critical mass. Prioritize the jobs to be done.

How to set and achieve goals

The opposite of failure, of course, is success—and success depends on achieving goals. Following are some ways to set and achieve your goals.

a. Understand and accept your limits and the limits of your people. Don't try to make a brain surgeon out of a good printer.

b. Break the big job down into manageable tasks. Remember, moving a mountain with a shovel requires you to do it one shovelful at a time. The biggest step is the first shovelful.

c. Don't allow "people conflicts" to sidetrack your energies. This includes problems with your boss or your spouse.

d. Forget self-indulgences. Sulking is a good way out, and avoiding the work and blaming the failure on someone else is a great way to reinforce your false sense of security.

e. Pick your best time. Some prefer A.M., some P.M. Learn to function at your personal peak. Don't leave it for day's end when you know that day's end is usually your end. Sometimes a short break is the best beginning to a tough job.

f. Decide if you need support and if so what kind. Don't wait so long to decide that you have to put together an ad hoc team. Your team will always work more efficiently if they have time to create or adjust to a plan.

g. Don't waste time in false preparation. Getting your desk cleared, for example, is an avoidance routine. Better to jump right in—the first shovelful is the toughest.

h. Recognize the signposts. If you can recognize the potential dangers, you can avoid the ultimate disasters. Think ahead.

Reach for the stars, land on the moon: But remember, reality is the key

Set your standards high in every case. You might not reach the ultimate in every case, but even when you fall somewhat short, your achievement will be substantial. You must, of course, be careful that you don't fall short so consistently as to create failure as your ultimate goal. The line between the two is a fine one and you must learn to recognize its proper place.

Examine your people, your equipment, and your other assets. Make a reasonable judgment as to the capability of the combination that will likely work best to accomplish the purpose. Ask the team to perform the maximum their competence appears likely to accomplish. Make the goal fit their capability. Asking them to do much more will create a frustration factor that could lead to lack of initiative, and ultimately to an energy level far short of that needed to accomplish the job. Don't run in front of their competence. Make sure the right team is in place. You will not find it easy to pick this fine line each time. As a builder of things, people, and teams, you must constantly reevaluate your thinking. With this experience, you can become the success builder.

Negotiation skills

Blinking is a sure sign of deception—not!

You will see books all over the bookstore shelves that tell you, "How to Read Your Adversary," "Don't Sit at the Head of the Table," and "Don't Give up Your Negotiating Strengths." You must be careful not to allow some of these clever titles to keep you from the basic goal of getting the job done. Some people blink faster or slower than others, and it has nothing to do with the stress they are under. Some people can sit in the same position for days; others can only tolerate the same position for minutes at a time. Some people cross their legs; others don't. Some people tap their fingers when they are holding four aces; others just raise the ante. Some people listen to music when they drive a car; some listen to talk shows; some don't turn on the radio. Be careful not to get caught up in word games that are much cuter than they are effective.

The glass top table

Once you've lost the trust of the party sitting on the other side of the table, you've got problems. If the buyer or seller believes you are hiding a material fact, whether inadvertently or intentionally, your ability to carry your argument to fruition is seriously impaired. It will take you a long time to reestablish this trust, and you will undoubtedly have lost momentum.

This chapter is not designed to be all things to all people in all situations. It is merely a reflection of the positive and negative attitudes that either foster or inhibit success and growth in the business marketplace. Consider these concepts as tools. Just as you will reach for one tool to do a particular job, you will reach for another to do a different kind of job. But keep the tools with you at every job site.

Take these tools with you to every business conference—even those conferences when you are merely talking with yourself. Some of those decisions are the most critical of all.

Key points

- Failure is not the end of the road. It is merely a stop on the journey. Make it a short stop—and move on.

- Discipline is not nearly as effective an incentive as the dollar.

- Maximize the creativity of your people by working on the idea "when it's hot."

- Excuses are the foundation posts of failure.

- Be careful not to get caught up in word games that are much cuter than they are effective.

Worksheet

- How has life in the business marketplace changed?

- When is failure an insidious predicate to future failures?

- Why is slowing down an idea a bad policy to follow?

- What is the best way to maximize your team's effort?

- What is the most important step in moving a mountain with a shovel?

7

Franchise or Otherwise

The necessary knowledge

In today's competitive marketplace, getting involved in business requires a good deal more than just a wing and a prayer. An entrepreneur must have a complete view of the business undertaking. This includes a knowledge of the history of the industry, the current competitive environment, and the future as it relates to innovations on the business horizon. Even more than this, the businessperson must understand the basic elements of the local marketplace, including adequacy of location, availability of competent personnel, advertising demographics, and the many aspects of competition.

All of this information is available to those who choose to seek it out. It is a complex search requiring at least the following: reading trade publications, discussing the industry with manufacturers and vendors and—perhaps the most significant examination of all— discussions with those already in the business. Unless you have this information under your belt, your business adventure can become seriously problematic.

Aside from the fundamental industry knowledge already noted, you will certainly need to understand the basics of operating a business. Your knowledge of accounting and law, however sparse, should serve as a starting point, suggesting when it would be necessary to seek the appropriate professional advice. In addition to these aspects of business operations, you will certainly want to have a minimum depth of knowledge with respect to the particular business on which your future will presumably depend, whether the business is manufacturing, food service, or printing.

Another way to go

There is another way to acquire this necessary knowledge. You can affiliate yourself with someone who has already acquired it. You could, for example, work for a company already in the business. This would at least give you the practical knowledge from a front line perspective. You could buy into a business as a partner, giving you a jump start in the industry. You would, of course, have to hope your partner has the knowledge you expect him or her to contribute. There is another very practical approach to solving this problem. You can buy a franchise.

When a company sells you a franchise, they essentially grant you a "permission." They will permit you to enjoy the knowledge and experience they have developed during their time in the industry. They will permit you to enjoy their reputation in the industry, normally acquired through advertising dollars spent in building their name, their trademarks, their logos—their recognition in the marketplace. They will permit you to take advantage of their quantity discounts with vendors, which they enjoy because of their ability to buy in bulk or make multiple purchases. The purchase of a franchise will eliminate most of the time that would normally be involved in searching for the above mentioned information. In addition, many of the elemental operational aspects of the business will be taught to you, eliminating, in great part, the myriad of mistakes normally made during the "on your own" learning period. Yes, there is a cost to all of this. But keep in mind that the question should not be "How much?" so much as it should be "What is the equivalent value to me in terms of the savings of time, energy, and potential error?" It requires a careful analysis.

The franchise method

Franchise companies are not normally interested in how much you, as a franchise candidate, know about the particular industry of which the franchise is a part. With the knowledge and experience they bring to the table, they feel they can give you a broad perspective on those aspects of the business. They also have the experience to teach you how to operate "the shop," whether it is a service business, a retail location, or a manufacturing or distribution operation. For the most part, this will usually be the case.

In today's business marketplace, there are some special characteristics franchise companies are looking for—people who can sell (and who enjoy selling) and people who can maintain attention to detail. Although both of these things can be taught, each requires an individual trait that must be inherent in the individual. Selling requires an inclination to put oneself in the face of rejection. Attention to detail requires a discipline and a willingness, to one degree or another, to conform to rules and regulations.

Franchising depends for its success, in great part, on the willingness of all franchisees (franchise owners) to conform to a game plan, to a pattern, to a method—some say, to "a look." It is in this "sameness" that the franchise is able to meet the expectations of its customers. Wherever the customer finds the franchise name or logo, he or she can expect similar surroundings, similar pricing and quality, and a consistency of product or service. Although every entrepreneur should be expected to exercise some degree of personal preference, the undisciplined franchisee who chooses not to conform can represent a clear danger to the continuity of the franchise. A loose cannon can destroy the concept.

The costs:
Today and tomorrow

The franchise company will have a franchise fee payable when you join the franchise. This will normally include your training, the company's help in finding an appropriate location in the marketplace of your choice, as well as a "kickoff" period during which franchise personnel will "hold your hand" while you go through your initial period of operation. In most franchises, this fee will also grant you some exclusivity with respect to a particular geography within which the franchise agrees it will not operate a similar franchise business nor will it authorize others to do so.

There will then be an ongoing payment, called a royalty or service fee, usually payable in monthly increments based on a percentage of your gross sales during the balance of the franchise contract. This payment is for ongoing support and education and is usually augmented by a secondary dollar contribution, also calculated on a percentage of gross sales in most cases. These secondary dollars are allocated to an advertising budget, either local or national or both.

Analyzing the dollars

You must examine the cost of the fee and determine if it will be "value for money" sufficient to warrant such an expenditure. You must decide if the reputation of the franchise will enhance your ability to grow the business. You must analyze the savings you will enjoy as the result of being a franchisee in terms of inventory or equipment purchasing power. You must evaluate the services you expect to receive on an ongoing basis in relation to what those services would cost if they were obtained from outside sources. You must essentially create a comparative analysis equation, which will ultimately help you decide if the costs—initially and on an ongoing basis—are consistent with your needs and expectations. The conservative position would certainly suggest that the franchise is a good "partner" if you have little knowledge about the industry or little experience in the operation of a similar business. Much, however, will depend on the franchise itself. Be sure to see Chapter 8, *Starting a Business or Buying One.*

Disclosure

Every company offering to sell a franchise anywhere in the United States must first, by law, give you a disclosure document. In some states, it is called a Uniform Franchise Offering Circular (UFOC). In other states, it is known as a Federal Disclosure Document. Beware of any company that discusses selling you a franchise without first offering you this document! This disclosure will tell you a great deal about the company, as well as give you information or sources of information from which you can obtain material relative to the industry itself. It will also disclose the history of the company, background on the people involved with the operation of the company, the financial stature of the company, a copy of the agreement you will be expected to sign, and a list of existing franchisees. It will give you plenty of things to think about and suggest additional sources (especially franchisees) from whom you might obtain important information. To ensure you totally understand both the financial and legal aspects of the disclosure, it is recommended you meet with your respective professionals to discuss its content.

Different things for different people

Each franchise offers different things to different people. Some will offer a complete accounting or inventory control system, which eliminates the need for this tedious aspect of an inventory-heavy business. Some will offer relationships with manufacturers or vendors, which will create advantages for your business that only many years on your own would otherwise accomplish. Some will offer constant training and keep you up to date on innovations in your industry. Some will give you immediate credibility or recognition in the marketplace that would otherwise take years to achieve. Some will offer secret formulas that protect the product you will be expected to offer. Each must be examined in the context of your personal needs and expectations.

Franchising is not for everyone. Some entrepreneurs need a great deal of help in initiating their business programs. Some need constant supervision to maintain continuing success. Some like to have someone looking over their shoulder or on whom they can rely in times of emergency. Some need to know they can rely on marketing and advertising savvy they themselves can't bring to the table.

The ice cream manufacturer's (franchisor's) dilemma

A franchisor of ice cream parlors was facing a serious problem with its franchisees. Sales had stopped growing; in fact, sales were dropping nationwide after the company had enjoyed decades of success and growth. Management hadn't paid much attention to changes in the marketplace because their revenues had maintained a fairly steady growth due to new franchise openings. When they finally recognized the stagnant revenues from normal ice cream sales, they realized they had not attended to their homework. They brought in some professionals to do an analysis of the marketplace. They were shocked at some of the results.

Four things had been happening in their industry to which they had not paid enough attention.

1. The high-calorie ice cream was suffering under the constant pressure of the new diet syndrome, which suggested healthy people should not be gaining weight.
2. Exotic flavors had been brought into the marketplace by a competitor who was doing a fantastic sales job on those for whom the diet syndrome played no part.
3. Yogurt had started to generate a much greater audience than it had ever enjoyed in previous years.
4. The supermarket chains had gotten much more aggressive in terms of the kinds of flavor, size, nonfat, and low-calorie alternatives they offered.

Recognizing the problem is one thing. Getting something done about it is always another. In this case, the franchisor wasted no time. They improved their assortment by including low-calorie ice cream, a whole new variety of flavors, and yogurt, including low-fat and nonfat. It was something that needed to be done expeditiously on behalf of their franchisees—and it was done.

The individual operator, whether a franchisee or an independent, might not have the personnel, the money, or the awareness to make so many changes in so short a period of time. The ultimate difference is that the franchise had the money to advertise this new "approach" to the entire nationwide community of customers. The individual operator would always find it difficult to allocate such substantial sums of money to so large an advertising campaign.

There are all kinds of franchise services to accommodate the different needs of the entrepreneur. The best advice is to carefully go over Chapter 4, *Looking in the Mirror,* and decide what kind of support you feel is necessary to best ensure your success. Then examine the franchises in the industry that attracts your attention; then do a comparative analysis of the franchise companies available; then ask franchisees and independent operators in the industry for their best judgment; then ask yourself again, "What is the equivalent value to me in terms of the savings in time, energy, and potential error?" You will be much closer to deciding if the cost of the franchise relationship has an equivalent in terms of your potential success.

Franchises—past and present

If a franchise is relatively new as a company, it is possible that you, as a member of a smaller group of franchisees, might get more personal attention. On the other hand, this advantage should be weighed against the franchisor's lack of significant experience in the marketplace. A franchisor that has been in the business for many years may be the better choice. A smaller franchise may have a tighter integrity and a closer relationship with its franchise owners, whereas a large franchise company may have a more significant visibility on the national scene.

As you examine the franchise "disclosure," you will note that all significant lawsuits will be discussed. An analysis of this litigation will suggest the kinds of problems the franchise company has had to deal with. It will also disclose any problems that were substantial enough to have caused a break in the franchisor-franchisee relationship. This relationship, aside from the specific services you will be offered, is an important element to consider. Remember, you will be expected to live up to the terms and conditions of the franchise contract, and any conflict will have to be resolved on the basis of mutual cooperation or end up in the courtroom.

You might also check the length of the franchise contract, during which you will be expected to observe and commit to the terms and conditions of the relationship. Be careful to note the conditions that will prevail following expiration of the contract. Will you be permitted to stay in business without operating under the franchise banner? Will you be permitted to keep your location? Will you be obliged to turn over the telephone number? How important do you consider these things to be?

As with any contractual relationship, you will want to completely understand your obligations during and after expiration of the contract. Since most legal language is subject to interpretation, and since many contracts are loaded with ambiguities in language, whether intentional or inadvertent, it is absolutely necessary that you seek professional advice before making any final judgment on which your future and the future of your family may depend.

Changing the contract

You may, as with any potential contract relationship, discuss with your counsel those items you find onerous or that might suggest the possibility of future problems.

Elements of most contracts are usually subject to negotiation. Keep in mind, however, that consistency is the very essence of franchising. To maintain and preserve any system where many people are part of a group and each is presumably equal to all others, there needs to be a basic contract relationship that is relatively the same in all cases. As each contract change is made, the equality among owners begins to wear thin. Each owner then begins to wonder if he or she got as good a deal as the other owners. These disparities will ultimately lead to bad feelings and a loss of the camaraderie so important to building and maintaining the integrity of the group.

Don't be surprised if the franchise contract is a difficult one in which to make changes. The consistency of the contract is part of the uniform nature of the franchise relationship throughout the group. If you feel you cannot live without certain changes, you should move on to a different franchise company. But, keep one last thing in mind. If the franchise company is easily convinced to make changes in your contract, you must then wonder what changes, significant or otherwise, might have been made in other contracts—and where do you stand in the line of preferential treatment?

Key points

- Understanding the specifics of the business as well as the industry of which the business is a part is the most important aspect of your quest for "the right thing."
- Make sure you "look in the mirror" and completely understand the talents you bring to the business—as well as the ones you don't.
- The franchise disclosure can answer many of the questions you will have about a particular business or industry.
- The best source of information will be the people who are already in the business.
- Make sure you do a comparative analysis of franchise services versus outside sources.

Worksheet

- What kinds of services are offered by a franchise?
- What is the purpose of the UFOC?
- Why is franchising not for everyone?
- What are franchise companies looking for in their buyer candidates?
- What will the litigation section of the disclosure document reveal?

8

Starting a Business versus Buying One

Conventional wisdom

It appears to be a general perception that the more money you invest in the purchase of a business, the bigger the business you will be able to buy. It also follows, if you subscribe to this conventional wisdom, that you will enjoy a larger personal income from the larger business' operation. It is very interesting that neither of these perceptions is valid.

What is more interesting is the fact that starting a new business—as opposed to buying an existing business—has much less conventional wisdom available, and there is good reason for this. If you are buying a new franchise, the franchise salesperson is likely to tell you the reasons why starting a new business is a better idea than buying an existing one. On the other hand, a business broker will likely suggest that an existing business will afford you a better opportunity for success. Do you wonder why the advice is different in each case?

Doing a comparative analysis

The fact is that a good comparison is almost impossible to make. In an existing business, its position in the marketplace can be examined from a variety of perspectives. All equipment currently being used for production can be compared to equipment in use by the competition. All sales elements—as well as the cost factors that support the sales—will have a history. Good and bad periods, customer variations, and seasonality fluctuations can all be carefully monitored. In other words, a potential buyer can get a pretty fair reading of the business by comparing its current profit picture with years—or at least months—of existing operations.

The new business is very different from an existing business. The entrepreneur can probably anticipate the business growth and the capital that will be necessary to get the business to its break-even point. This can be done by comparing the business to others of similar size and activity in the particular industry of which the business is a part. However, there are many elements that will not allow any serious degree of reliability in the use of such a comparison. After all, the city in which the business is situated may not have sufficient similarities to make the comparison valid. The particular location, especially for a retail operation, is often a defining cause of success, and one location may not be equivalent to another for a variety of reasons. The effect of competition, although clearly defined in relation to the existing business, may be very unclear until the new business actually makes its intrusion into the competitive marketplace.

If the new business sounds to you like an outright gamble, as opposed to the more calculated risk of an existing operation, you would not be far from wrong. It is a historically sound axiom that buying an existing business will usually cost no more and, in many cases, will cost less than an equivalent business started from scratch. The simplest reason is that the existing operation has a recognizable cost-to-sales ratio. That is, the cost of generating the sales will likely have been maintained within acceptable limits, or else the business would probably not be viable. In a new venture, the cost of doing business will be a day-to-day drain on working capital before the reservoir of working capital can be replenished by sufficient sales to accommodate the cost. The length of time it takes to achieve this equilibrium requires cash.

The tradeoffs are significant

The positive side of starting a new business is that you can start on the proverbial shoestring, even operating, in some cases, at the beginning, as a home-based business. The rent factor can be eliminated as an initial cost of doing business. Also, equipment can be rented for the periods required, as opposed to a purchase or a long-term lease commitment. The rental aspect may be a little more costly in the short term, but it allows for a generous flexibility and a more judicious use of the limited working capital available.

Many business functions can be outsourced as needed, as opposed to having permanent personnel available at a constant cost, together with the concurrent amenities that might be standard features of employment in the industry. The entrepreneur can handle many business functions early on that will later be allocated to outside sources or inside personnel at an additional cost as profits become available for these purposes. There are, therefore, as always, tradeoffs that must be considered before such a judgment is made.

Looking more carefully at the component parts
Fewer answers

In Chapter 7, *Franchise or Otherwise*, you were able to compare the comfort zone available to a franchisee versus the "learning on your own" concept. The differentials in this chapter are not much different. If you choose to start a business from scratch, you will have many of the same questions you might have if you bought an existing operation. The difference is, as you've seen, that in a new venture you will have fewer answers.

Location

If you are contemplating a retail business, whether you will be selling products or services, you will need to examine locations on a comparative basis. You will need to examine space and cost to determine whether your anticipated sales revenue can be produced in the allocated space and whether that same sales revenue can afford the price of that space. In an existing business, the ratio of cost to sales is already a known factor.

Personnel, etc.

In a new venture, you will have to analyze your personnel requirements for internal operations such as salespeople, equipment operators, and the like. You will also have to examine those functions that can be outsourced, such as bookkeeping, legal, accounting, and perhaps outside sales. In an ongoing business, these functions and related costs are already part of the picture, and you can easily examine them.

However, be especially careful about the longevity of existing personnel after your purchase and takeover of a business. If the business is dependent on one or more key people, you will need some assurance that these people will remain with the business. The loss of such a person, or people, could be disastrous to the continuity of the business. Further, what if this person were involved in sales, having a direct relationship with one or more important customers?

What if this person decided not only to leave the business but to join the competition? What effect is this likely to have on your business? Are there any ways to protect against such a defection?

Tom and Shelley Bromwell in Anchorage, Alaska certainly faced this problem in dramatic fashion. Over a period of eleven years, they lost three salespeople, each of whom went to work for the competition. In each case, the defector took ten to twenty percent of the business to the competitor. Each time, the loss of business caused a cash flow problem. It is fortunate this business was successful enough and the cash reservoir was big enough to handle this problem until an equivalent amount of business could be generated. Not every business has this luxury of additional dollars to cope with such an emergency. In many instances, such an event could easily destroy the business.

After getting some professional advice, Tom and Shelly decided to establish a deferred compensation plan with each of their salespeople. The agreement provided for a portion of their income (together with an amount contributed by the company) to be put into a separate escrow (holding) account. When employees leave the job, this money will be paid to them over a period of time, providing they do not go to work for a competitor in the area during that designated period. There are a variety of ways this can be implemented, but this is the core element of the concept. And it works.

Many companies use a "covenant not to compete" in their employment contract. A covenant not to compete is designed to prevent such a disaster from happening. It is an agreement by which the employee promises not to compete with the business after leaving the job. Do you think a covenant not to compete signed by the employee is a good idea? Do you think this is enforceable in court in your particular state? Do you think a deferred compensation agreement is a better idea? Would you think that discussing this with the appropriate professional is a good idea?

Understanding your capital requirements

The most important element—aside from the validity of the concept and the competitive position of the product or service in the marketplace—is money.

In a new business venture, you will need to make preliminary judgments relative to the amount of capital you will need for various items. Rent, personnel, equipment, inventory, advertising, legal services, accounting, and your own living expenses are just a few of the business aspects that will require working capital.

Even in an existing business, you will need to make an assessment as to your working capital requirements. The simplest reason for this is the concept of the "receivable turnover period." If a successful company wants to buy your product or service but pays its bill ninety days after delivery, you will likely agree to provide the product or service. However, you will need to have cash in the bank during this waiting period. You will have to buy raw materials, and pay your rent, personnel, and other administrative expenses during this period before your receivable turns over into cash.

Handling the growth problem

This preliminary assessment will be designed to take you to your first plateau—survival. It is interesting that business success, usually evidenced by growth, will require additional capital. Growth will often surpass your original capacity to produce.

Growth might cause you to consider a larger location, more equipment, additional or more specialized personnel, a more diverse inventory, or advertising over a larger geographical territory. Dynamic growth might even cause you to contemplate an entirely different delivery system, such as additional locations or franchising. This kind of growth will demand even more capital.

The best way to anticipate this kind of problem—and, make no mistake, it is exactly the kind of problem that most entrepreneurs dream of having—is to do a periodic appraisal of your business goals. This means you must have a plan, a road map, to see where you've been, where you are, and where you're going. You might want to look at Chapter 2, *Getting the Money,* Chapter 3, *The Business Plan*, and Chapter 10, *More on Investors and Partners.*

The advantage to buying

The advantage to buying an existing business is you will be able to assess the costs, competition, and other elements of the sales picture as they exist at the time of purchase. You will have an idea of where the business can go based on where the business has been. You will have fewer questions unanswered and you will probably have a pretty good idea of what the activities and profit should be over a given period of time.

How much money will you need?

Buying an existing business should hold fewer surprises. The cash flow of the business you buy should be able to take care of you, the buyer, and it should be able to pay the balance of the purchase price. In other words, *the business should be able to buy itself.*

You should be sure to completely understand this concept. Remember, very few businesses are purchased for cash. The prevailing statistic shows that most businesses are bought with a down payment, say twenty percent of the purchase price, with the balance of the price being paid over a period of five to ten years. Since most people use most of their available capital to buy the business, it is essential that the cash flow of the business itself be available to take care of the buyer's family as well as to meet the payment obligations on the balance of the purchase price. For more on this concept, you will want to read Chapter 18, *How to Value a Business.*

Starting a new venture

When you start a new venture, whether it is an independent or a franchise, you will need to get the operation to its break-even point as your first order of business. In fact, this becomes the first plateau you need to reach, and the achievement of this goal will depend in great part on your having the necessary capital available to get there.

The amount of money you will need to get to "break-even" will, of course, be different in different businesses. To start a lemonade stand does not require the kind of investment necessary to start a software manufacturing company. The equipment is different, the approach to the customer is different, and the profits are certainly more conjectural in the one than in the other.

Setting your own style

Many businesses are susceptible to being developed along considerably different lines. A food business can serve various kinds of food, or it can devote its menu to a single palate. Some Mexican restaurants serve only Mexican food. Some also serve Italian food. Some restaurants noted for hamburgers also serve tacos. Some clothing stores carry a line only for women, some only for children, and some only petite sizes. By buying a business, you are buying its position in the marketplace. Yes, you can change its direction, but don't forget the basics. If you buy an existing business, you are doing so because it has already established its niche, its position in the marketplace. If you disturb this strength, you may weaken its position. You might even destroy it. Then what purpose was served? What you really should do is capitalize on its strength. If your intention is to divert its direction to a different product line, then perhaps you ought to reconsider the acquisition. You might be better advised to start a business from scratch. Be careful about understanding the goal you need to reach.

Other reasons for acquisition

There are, as always, exceptions to this rule. Sometimes a business is purchased not to maintain its continuity, but merely to acquire its geographical location. In other instances, the business may be bought because it is synergistic to another existing business already owned by the buyer. In yet other cases, the business may be an exciting proposition because you are acquiring a particularly good staff, or a specially trained or knowledgeable person, or even the owner, who may have excellent contacts in the industry you choose to enter.

In today's technological business environment, creativity is a sought after commodity. The computer has created a plethora of categories in which software development is a never ending source of new ideas on which businesses are predicated and built. However, buying a business to acquire the genius—either the idea or the individual who created it—might not end up being a bed of roses.

Creators think their ideas are their own. Businesses that pay the creator's salary think the idea (created during the periods of the creator's paydays) belongs to the business. Legal cases on this problem have gone both ways. Do not think that a contract defining this problem is the answer. Contract language is subject to ambiguity and interpretation. The conception of the idea is quite subjective and difficult to position in time. The question "Was the idea developed during the week or on the weekend?" will give you some idea as to the magnitude and complexity of this problem. Litigation to resolve this dilemma is time consuming and costly even when successful. Another question to be considered is, "You can make the basketball player get on the court, but can you make him play well? A good strategy for dealing with the acquisition of a creative person is a fairness doctrine that will both motivate the creator and enhance his or her relationship with the company. See your professional before you embark on such an acquisition.

Key points

- Be careful that your comparative analysis deals with sufficient similarities to warrant following the course of the original business.

- Make sure your working capital availability is sufficient, whether you are contemplating starting a new business or acquiring an existing one.

- Look at the history of an existing business to get some idea about its potential after a takeover.

- Be careful to understand the role existing personnel play in the business.

- Be careful not to take over a successful business and then completely change its reason for having become successful.

Worksheet

- What is the danger of relying too heavily on a comparative analysis?

- What is the first plateau that should be reached in your new business?

- Why is it normally a safer route to buy a business as opposed to starting one?

- How can you make an assessment of the working capital required in buying an existing business? in starting a new business?

- What is the danger in acquiring a creative person as part of your acquisition?

9

Dealing with the Professionals

In today's complex business marketplace, it is impossible to understand all the elements of operating a business. It is necessary to reach out for advice to those who are expert in their respective fields.

The language of the professionals

The difference between an option to renew and a right of first refusal in a lease may be second nature to the transactional lawyer, but it is hardly normal fare for the average businessperson. Understanding all the purposes to be served by a general ledger, a balance sheet, and a profit and loss statement requires an in-depth study of accounting that is not in the background of many small business people. (See Chapter 12, *Understanding Your Income Statement.*) The process of breaking down a demographic profile in order to take maximum advantage of radio, television, or print media advertising is the daily activity of the advertising agency, but is not part of the daily activity of the entrepreneur. (See Chapter 13, *Marketing and Advertising.*) The real question is, How much of this information is needed to properly maintain the continuity of the business?

Dire consequences

If you are in a retail business, you will certainly need to understand your product and how you can generate enough profit from its sales to survive and prosper in the marketplace, but other things are also important.

In your lease, for example, you may not need to understand a *right of first refusal* if you have no intention of buying the property in which your business functions, but you will certainly need to know the terms and conditions relating to your *option to renew* for an additional period at the expiration of your original lease term. See Chapter 11, *Contracts and Leases*. To ensure that you completely understand the conditions under which you are entitled to exercise your option to renew and whether or not the increased rental will allow you to maintain your business and its profit structure, you would be wise to seek the advice of a lawyer. The money you spend for a careful analysis may be very minor compared to the problems you may face because you didn't completely understand the changes orchestrated by the language of the lease. Thinking you understand the language of the professionals may lead to dire consequences if in fact you don't!

An option to renew "on the same terms and conditions of the original lease" is considerably different than an option to renew on terms and conditions to be negotiated at the time of renewal. The latter is not an option to renew at all. It is merely an opportunity to discuss and negotiate, failing which you will not have a lease at all. Doing business from the street is not an option!

Paying the piper

Because of the constantly changing aspects of taxes on almost every level—federal, state, and local—it would seem that relying on the professional to properly compute and file your taxes is a good idea, saving time and, more often than not, money as well.

On the other hand, it is necessary for you to understand the picture you are looking at when examining your income statement so you can properly deal with the constantly changing aspects of your business. You'll need to be able to do this yourself. Think about the following example.

> If there has been a change in your operating profit because your cost of product increased during a given period of time, it is essential you examine each line item to determine the specific reason for each cost increase. This would let you correct the problem before it permanently affects your profit structure. Following the line item to its core and finding, for example, that you have not been charging for "pickup and delivery" can suggest that this "new cost" be added to the price of the product, leaving the profit as it existed previously. Not recognizing this cost increase may lead to the demise of your business—and you'll never even know why!

As you examine your marketing analysis and decide just what advertising might be most appropriate in your judgment, you will still be better served by discussing this with your marketing professional. His or her experience, together with constantly changing demographic information, will enable you to take advantage of the most cost-effective approach to informing your customer base about your product or service.

Caution!

Although it is certainly appropriate, if not necessary, to seek the counsel of the professional to ensure your own decisions are "on target," keep in mind that they should be *your* decisions. Many professionals become so interested in the business they represent that they are often inclined to advise the entrepreneur on those things about which they have little knowledge, thinking perhaps their instincts are better than yours. Take advantage of their advice with respect to their field of knowledge, but do not let them encroach on business judgments. These are the meat and potatoes of your daily activity, and you undoubtedly are more knowledgeable in this area than they are. Be especially careful when the lawyer gives you advice about marketing or the advertising executive gives you advice on accounting. You must be the conduit through which all this advice flows, and it must be tempered constantly with your understanding of the realities of your business and your particular trade or industry.

Another piper to pay!

Whatever your product or service may be, you will invariably be quoting prices to your customers. In fact, in many businesses, there is a published price list. Certainly, if your customer asks you what the price is going to be, even in situations where you must figure and quote an estimate, the question is not cause for embarrassment. In most businesses, the consumer wants to know the price to factor it into his or her business' budget. Why, then, is it so difficult to ask the same question of a professional? The fact of the matter is that it shouldn't be. You need to anticipate the cost for your own budget, whether it be the cost of a collection action, incorporation of the business, analysis of a lease or contract, clarification of a tax matter, examination of your income statement, preparation of a media campaign, or production of a television commercial...and on and on it goes. You need to know the cost prior to making a commitment to know if your business can afford the product or service.

In some cases, it is not possible to quote an exact price because the professional often works on the basis of his or her time. It is, however, the obligation of the professional to understand that all costs must be properly programmed into the business' budget, and in that context he or she ought to be able to give you an estimate either on the basis of time or project. At the very worst, you ought to be able to get the high and the low estimate depending on the nature of the project and the extent to which you would to become obligated.

For goodness' sake, don't be embarrassed about asking what the time of your professional will cost!

The language differential

The real problem in dealing with your professionals is the problem of communication.

> Alvin Brownell was in the hospital waiting room to find out if his dad was going to survive a recent emergency. The surgeon came into the waiting area and addressed Alvin and the other members of the family. He spoke distinctly but quickly. "Your father has just suffered a myocardial infarction. If he can survive the next 24 hours, we may be able to celebrate his next birthday." Then he turned and walked away.

Whether the doctor thought he was being informative or otherwise is unimportant. The fact is that the family, under the tremendous pressure of a potential personal loss, was hardly in a position to interpret or understand this "insider" language.

> Alvin called the surgeon back and, in no uncertain terms, told him what he thought of the doctor's short, somewhat cryptic description of his father's condition. The surgeon's response was immediate. "Mr. Brownell, I apologize. It was unthinking of me. I'm glad you stopped me. And I can assure you, it will never happen again. Unfortunately, among ourselves, we have gotten used to 'shortcut language' that patients and family find difficult to understand. It is our shortcoming and a bad one." He then proceeded to explain to Alvin and the family just what this "heart attack" meant and why the next 24 hours would be critical.

When a doctor uses the term "myocardial infarction" instead of "heart attack," we can easily see the problem involved in "failure to communicate."

The problem usually starts with the professional. In many cases, he or she is so used to dealing with others in the same profession that the vocabulary used may include a great deal of peer language with which the layperson is unfamiliar. In their own professional circles or in the office with associates in the business, this peer language represents a "shortcut" to communicating. This shortcut, however, can be a real problem for the client who does not understand the basic connotations, let alone the subtleties involved.

If you owned a print shop, for example, and used terminology—about etching plates, watermarks on paper, or certain types of ink—peculiar only to the trade, the customer would be quite "put off" at being in a situation that reflects his or her ignorance of the subject. You would want to avoid doing this because your relationship with your customer is important. You would likely use language common to both of you or, in the event a reference to a trade term was necessary, you would try to explain it, being careful not to demean the intelligence of the customer.

It is the professional's obligation to ensure that you, as the client, fully understand the import of his or her advice. Remember, the purpose of your visit to the professional is to get a clear understanding of the meaning of words unfamiliar to you. And you are paying for this education. In some cases, the professional may even be able to examine with you certain language that contains ambiguities. Although it is not always possible to develop a clear definition to counter such ambiguities, you will at least be able to discuss the alternatives with someone who has faced such ambiguities in the past and who understands the variety of ways many have been resolved. As with so many other things in the business world, being prepared is a good position to be in when problems arise.

If your professional's advice leaves you with a lack of understanding or with questions not answered to your satisfaction, STOP! Make sure your problem of communication is resolved. If he or she cannot develop a lay language that allows both of you to read from the same sheet of music, as the old saying goes, then you'd better get another professional who can. The simple fact of the matter is that there are very few things in the business world that cannot be explained in simple, lay language. Even the most complex subject can be broken down into its component parts, have each of the parts examined and explained, and be put back together again.

The best way to find an appropriate professional is to ask people you know and on whose opinions you are willing to rely. Their recommendation is probably the best you can get. If you need to interview a professional, it's a good idea to find out about the essence of his or her practice. A lawyer who specializes in criminal trial work is probably not the best candidate to represent you in the purchase of a business. Find out if the lawyer has had any experience in the particular industry you are examining. In the event you are examining a franchise, ask about any franchise situations the lawyer has handled. An ideal situation would be to have the lawyer suggest that you contact one of his or her former clients for whom the lawyer has handled a similar situation. Whichever professional you choose, make sure he or she is able to communicate with you on your level of expertise.

Don't let any professional tell you myocardial infarction has no alternative in terms of explanation. It is merely a heart attack!

Key points

- Failure to understand "terms and conditions" of a document can shorten the life of your business.

- You would expect your professional to satisfy your questions just as you would satisfy the questions of your customer.

- Failure to communicate clear meaning is the fault of the professional, not you.

- A complex problem should be broken down into its component parts.

- If your professional can't communicate with you, get another professional.

Worksheet

- Why do you need to visit with your various professionals?

- Why should you ask about the professional's fee in advance and discuss the parameters of his or her advisory capacity?

- What could the problem be if you don't understand an "option to renew?"

- Why do you need to go over the individual line items on your income statement?

- How best can a complex question be answered?

The following is a letter of engagement by an accountant for tax preparation:

∽∾

Dear Charles:

This letter is to confirm and specify the terms of my engagement with you and to clarify the nature and extent of the services I will provide. In order to ensure an understanding of our mutual responsibilities, I ask all clients for whom returns are prepared to confirm the following arrangements.

I will prepare your tax returns from information you will furnish me. I will not audit or otherwise verify the data you submit. It is your responsibility to provide all the information required for the preparation of complete and accurate returns. You have the final responsibility for the income tax returns; therefore, you should review them carefully before you sign them.

I will use professional judgment in resolving questions where the tax law is unclear. Unless otherwise instructed by you, I will resolve such questions in your favor whenever possible. I am not an attorney, however, and cannot provide you with legal opinions or analysis of these positions. If you desire a legal opinion before choosing among alternative tax positions, then legal counsel should be separately retained for this purpose.

Your returns may be selected for review by the tax authorities. I will be available upon request to represent you and will render additional invoices for the time and expense incurred.

My fee for these services will be based upon the amount of time required at standard billing rates, plus out-of-pocket expenses. All invoices will be due and payable upon presentation.

If the foregoing fairly sets forth your understanding, please sign the enclosed copy of this letter in the space indicated and return it to my office.

Yours very truly,

Eddie Murphy, CPA

Accepted:

_____   _____
Signature of Client   Date

Note the language that covers (a) inaccuracy of financial information submitted by the client; (b) ultimate responsibility for the accuracy of the return before submitting to the government; (c) responsibility for any legal opinions, and (d) additional fees for services to be rendered in the event of an audit.

There is nothing wrong with any of this protective language. The only comment made by the author is that the letter appears to be drafted exclusively for the benefit of the accountant, and not in any way for the protection or even edification of the client.

Also, note that the letter does not define "standard billing rates" nor does it discuss what exactly would comprise "out-of-pocket" expenses. Would you want to know what these are? Would you want to know what the approximate cost might be based on your particular financial portfolio?

The following is a letter of engagement by a business consultant for the valuation and possible subsequent representation of the client relative to the sale of the business.

Dear Charles:

This letter will serve to define our relationship relative to the valuation and sale of your business located at 1224 Spine Court, in Appleberg, Minnesota.

Since I will be doing a basic financial analysis of your business for valuation, I will be depending on the accuracy of the financial statements presented to me for that purpose. I will, of course, not be accepting any responsibility for the validity of those statements. Anything outside the financial paperwork presented will not be included unless otherwise noted.

You will be paying me a retainer of $1,500 for the first day plus any and all expenses incurred with respect to travel, hotels, meals, and incidentals. Any additional time will be billed at $200/hour. It is anticipated that the basic valuation (a selling price for the business) can be done in one day. If you need an additional written valuation for presentation purposes (often used for court purposes), this will likely take an additional four to five hours. This additional cost should not exceed $1,000 unless there is reason for it to be more extensive than the original calculations, i.e., requiring an examination of the industry, competitive analysis, or the like.

You may decide to work with me to sell the business after the valuation is finished instead of working with a broker. In that event you should be aware that my hourly fee of $200 per hour will still pertain. This, of course, is in lieu of the broker's fee (normally 10–12% of the selling price), since I don't take a commission on sale. In the event you want me to qualify each buyer, the time on the phone is about 20 minutes. This would equate to about $65 per call. If the buyer shows a sincere interest, suggesting a more extensive conversation, the cost would be proportionate to the time spent.

There is no way to determine a specific price for my representation due to the conjectural nature of the time required. My track record will give you reason to make a positive comparison. If your business sells for $500,000, then the commission payable to a broker will be $50,000–$60,000. If we worked for an entire year, it is unlikely that my fee would exceed one-half of this figure. On the other hand, you will be obligated to pay my fee whether you sell the business or not. The broker's commission is usually payable only on sale. This is a choice that you must make.

I would appreciate your signing this letter and returning a signed copy to me indicating that you understand the terms of our working relationship. You will note that there is no time limit to this relationship. It should last only as long as you are satisfied that I am performing to your best advantage. You may cancel the arrangement at any time and you will be expected to pay only for the time and expenses already accrued.

Please let me know if you have any additional questions.

Cordially,

Ira N. Nottonson

Understood, acknowledged, and agreed to:

_____   _____

Signature of Client   Date

Do you find this letter to be more specific than the former?

Does it sound any friendlier than the first?

Does it sound less intimidating?

What additional information would you like to have?

Do you think you will have any problem getting additional information?

Is there anything about the terms you don't understand?

Does there appear to be any embarrassment at mentioning the cost of the services?

There is no arbitration clause in either letter. Do you think there should be?

What kinds of "contract relationships" do you think should contain such a clause?

10

More on Investors
and Partners

The concept of "giving up control" was examined briefly in Chapter 2, *Getting the Money*. The problems, however, are so deeply rooted and so potentially devastating that a second, more careful scrutiny is clearly in order. The primary goal of the average entrepreneur is to be "captain of his ship and master of his destiny." This certainly suggests that he or she expects to set the goals, chart the course, and maintain continuity until the goal has been achieved.

Everybody answers to somebody

The problem is that the worker answers to the boss, the V.P. answers to the president, the CEO answers to the board of directors, and the entrepreneur must ultimately answer to the customer. The question is, apart from the customer, who else will the entrepreneur need to examine business decisions with before they can be implemented? The answer will normally be an investor or a partner.

What tools are in the toolbox?

A well worn business axiom the business owner would do well to remember is "diamonds are forever; partnerships are not!" On the other hand, not only can a partnership be a positive format with which to initiate a business but, in some cases, it is the only way a business can be moved out of the starting blocks. Each person comes to the table with certain basic skills and with some experience. It would be unusual for anyone to have acquired *all* the tools necessary to properly operate a business in almost any trade or industry. The exception might be the person who has, early on, decided on a life's work and studied and worked toward this single goal starting early in life. One example might be a surgeon. Another example might be be a surgeon. Another example might be a son or daughter who has been brought up in the business and trained by the mother or father for ultimate family succession.

For the most part, however, this will not be the case. The average entrepreneur will find that the business' toolbox is missing a number of important items. It is then necessary, in one way or another, to acquire these tools. Such an acquisition can be made by affiliating with someone who has the tools. We might then be talking about a partnership.

Joint venture

In the business world, you have undoubtedly heard the words "joint venture" many times. Many "beginners" are put off because it really sounds like something special. It isn't. A joint venture is exactly what it sounds like. It is a combination of two or more people embarking on a business venture. It can take the form of a partnership, a corporation, or any of the other legal entities covered in more detail in Chapter 21, *Legal Entities*. Each person can put in the same dollar investment, or the investment can vary from joint venturer to joint venturer. Sometimes two or more mature companies can participate in a joint venture. Sometimes it can be a horizontal joint venture—that is, companies on the same level doing the same thing, such as two retail stores. Sometimes, it can be a vertical joint venture; that is, companies on different levels doing different things, such as a manufacturer and a retailer. Each will presumably have something of value to contribute, in return for which each will expect a reward of some kind, usually in the context of money or discounts that will ultimately convert to dollars.

Partnership synergy

The partnership is probably the most prevalent of the joint venture concepts. A partnership can be composed of two or more people. In some cases, the partners will contribute equal dollars to initiate or buy a business. But this does not have to be the case. In some cases, an individual with technical or mechanical expertise will "partner" with an individual with marketing or financial abilities. It is the synergy of two different backgrounds that will, in most cases, be the predicate for a successful partnership. In still other cases, the partnership may be made up of one individual with the expertise in the particular business and another with the money to fund the business and allow the first partner to function in the business marketplace.

Active or passive

A combination of partners may not necessarily have both working in the business. One may be an active participant; the other, who may have contributed the money, may be passive, that is, not actually work in the business. In fact, in many cases, in the early days of a business one partner (this may also be a husband or a wife) will continue to work outside the business until the business can afford to meet the salary requirements of both partners. This concept of a passive partner begins to mirror the concept of investors. But, before examining that aspect, take a look at the negative side of the partnership.

Diamonds are forever...

It is certainly difficult enough for even husbands and wives—and marriage is the highest embodiment of the partnership concept—to agree on all things all the time. Consider, then, two individuals spending most of their waking hours working on the goal of creating a business success. Would you expect them to agree on all things all the time? Clearly not. How then are these conflicts—these failures to agree on the concept, direction, or specifics of the business—to be resolved? Most of the time the conflicts are relative to a minor problem and will usually be answered by virtue of one partner having more expertise in that area than the other. Sometimes resolution comes when one partner decides it is not worth pursuing the conflict at the risk of creating a problem in the personal relationship between the two. Sometimes the conflict may require an arbitrator, and sometimes the conflict may, unfortunately, have a long-term, negative impact on the partnership relationship.

The worst of these problems could conceivably cause a serious breach in the partnership, resulting in both parties recognizing they can no longer work together. In some cases, loss of one partner can actually cause the business to falter or fail. This contingency must be anticipated, and adequate preparation must be made at the beginning of the relationship to handle this potential problem between the partners without the business being destroyed as a result of the conflict.

Other contingencies must also be anticipated. Very often, at the beginning of a partnership, an insurance policy might be taken out on both partners, allowing the business to survive in the event of the untimely death of either partner. The idea of conflict must be approached from this same perspective. After all, the goal (at least in part) was for the partners to protect and grow their investment, whether of time, energy, creativity, or dollars. The destruction of the business will deny all partners any possible equity that might have been earned during the life of the partnership.

The buyout concept

To avoid any such permanent damage, the original partnership contract should contain a method by which one or the other of the partners can exit the company without destroying the business. This can be done in a variety of ways, one of which would be to agree to a formula for buyout purposes that can be applied at any time either partner desires to leave. Arrangements, of course, must be made to replace the missing partner and his or her expertise to ensure continuity of the business. In the case of a passive partner, arrangements must be made for a return of dollars and possibly distribution of profits based on the earned equity existing at the time of the partnership breakup. The agreement should be careful to ensure that the money taken from the business does not leave the company with insufficient working capital to maintain its operation. You will find that even though it may never be necessary to use any such "contingency language," it will at least serve to alleviate any pressures caused by conflict during the course of the relationship.

The investor or lender

The investor or lender gives a different cast to the problem. The day-to-day conflict resulting from working closely together may create conflict, but it could be worse. The working partners may differ with respect to any particular aspect of the day-to-day business approach, but it is likely that their goals will be the same because they both understood the initial dream. The investor or lender, on the other hand, may understand the long-term goal but may be much more conservative regarding how that goal is achieved. Investors may express this by watching the dollars too closely in the short term. This kind of attitude can be devastating to the entrepreneur, who recognizes that very often the biggest dollars have to be spent in the early days. The "second guessing" aspect of the investor or lender can be inimical not only to the entrepreneur but, ultimately, to the lenders or investors themselves.

All of this must be considered at the outset of the relationship and taken into account when the decision is made as to who will be responsible for what kinds of judgments or expenditures relative to actual operation of the business. With a clear understanding at the outset, minor as well as major problems and conflicts can be avoided. Do not take for granted that "everything will probably work out." If it is not specifically delineated, the odds are that it probably "will not!"

Value for money

The real question you must ask, in any situation where your decision making may be subject to someone else's thinking, is whether the introduction of a third party—for any reason—is going to be worth it. More money will certainly allow for accelerated growth, but "enough" money will allow you to get started without anticipating any interference. Technical or marketing expertise might give you great comfort in the decisions you need to make to move the business forward, but there are negatives to consider as well.

A partner can service this need, but the same expertise is probably available at a price outside the business. Your question should be, Which is the best way to fulfill short-term and long-term goals? If you don't have the money, a partner will be ideal in the short term. Remember, however, a partner will have an interest in the long-term rewards as well. Which direction would you prefer to take in your business?

Using the experience of others

There is, of course, another side to this issue. It is fair to say that however expert you may be with respect to the business you own, it is impossible to anticipate the myriad of problems that will evidence themselves on any given day or in any given period of time. There could be shortages in available inventory, precipitous price changes, dynamic changes in competition, or new equipment becoming available. Any one or more of these would be impossible to anticipate and any one could dramatically affect your business, either in the short term or the long term. Without the years of experience in facing changes of this nature, you can often be left in a position where a wrong decision could entirely alter your business' prospects for continuity or success.

By having partners, lenders, or investors at your shoulder, you have people with experience other than your own who can contribute to your decision making and help you step over these unexpected hurdles, allowing the business to maintain itself. Certainly, you could solicit advice from any number of professionals. You could even put together—as many companies do—an outside board of directors which, by its varied experience, can be helpful in making appropriate business judgments. However, people who already have a vested interest in your future, and in their own as well, will likely spend more time helping you make a value decision than the outsider whose help is really momentary until they get in a car or on a plane to go home. The other side of that argument, however, is that since they don't have a personal involvement, their thinking may prove to be more objective. Which would you think is the better advice? Would you think that the kind of problem to be solved might play a big part in your answer?

It is this kind of alternative you must factor into the positives and negatives of partners, investors, and lenders. Whatever your decision, make sure the parameters of the relationship are clearly set out in language that is well defined and unambiguous. It will put you on a much clearer road to the goals you've chosen.

Remember also the "exit strategies" discussed in Chapter 2, *Getting the Money.*

Key points

- Make sure the partnership synergy is valuable enough to warrant sharing the equity.
- Draft your agreements to ensure continuity of the business in the event of conflict.
- Determine the degree of control you will be giving up for the investor's participation.
- Discuss "early on" the working parameters involved in each person's part of the business.
- Don't give up your long-term goals merely for short-term convenience.

Worksheet

- What is the value of taking on a partner?
- When is it appropriate to examine the agreement between partners?
- Why is it necessary to establish a formula to value the business in the event of a partnership conflict?
- What purpose can investors serve in addition to their financial support?
- What will you look for when you "look in the mirror" before making these decisions?

11

Leases and Contracts

Basic language

To do business in today's marketplace, it is essential you understand some basic aspects of a business relationship. Unless you are a practitioner of the law, it is unlikely that you will understand the entire spectrum of legal language. It is possible, however, for you to have a handle on many of the fundamentals. With this basic sense of the contract relationship, you should be able to develop a workable vocabulary. Without these basics, you are likely to find yourself vulnerable to those who are anxious to take advantage.

The first lesson to be learned is that there is nothing so complex that it must remain a well kept secret to all but those few who are legally indoctrinated. If that were the case, many in the American business marketplace would be unable to cope and the marketplace would collapse. Such is obviously not the case. As with any difficult problem (or sentence), the idea is to break it down into its component parts, examine and understand the meaning of each part, and then reassemble the whole. The whole will invariably become more understandable.

There is nothing—conceptually, philosophically, or otherwise—that cannot be broken down into simple language. Anyone who suggests otherwise is being less than honest, or perhaps they themselves have a problem with the basic concept of communication. Don't ever be embarrassed into believing that you can't understand. If your professional can't explain it adequately, get another professional (see Chapter 9, *Dealing with Professionals*).

Oral contracts

Every legal jurisdiction—usually designated by state—has slightly different laws about many aspects of business. In some states, for example, an oral contract is not valid if it is for a value in excess of $500. In most jurisdictions, any transfer of real property must be in writing to be valid. It is always appropriate to check with your lawyer to examine the law of your particular jurisdiction.

The most important thing to remember is that resolving an oral contract invariably depends on the ability of the arbiter (the judge, the jury, the mediator) to discern which of the parties is telling the truth. Truth, therefore, is essentially based on credibility. The problem is that some people (telling the truth or otherwise) appear to be more credible than others. It is wise to depend on the written word carefully structured at the outset of a relationship rather than trying to resolve ambiguities after unclear language becomes a problem.

Handling the non-contract

If it is deemed inappropriate or unnecessary by one of the parties to document the business relationship, it would be wise for the other party to keep a running narrative. Although it would certainly be called self-serving by the party who wanted to deny its validity, courts are very inclined to accept notes made contemporaneously to an event.

The more such notes that are kept, the more difficult it is for the other side to suggest deniability. It is interesting that such notes are often able to resurrect vague memories, especially when the failure to remember is really a question of bad memory and not bad faith. It is also a good idea to share these notes with the other party. Failure of the other party to deny the comments in timely fashion often suggests to a finder of fact that the narrative was accepted by both parties. In some cases, when it is appropriate, some people even put the following language at the close of the narrative: "If I do not hear from you to the contrary, I will assume that the above is a fair representation of our discussions to date." You can certainly see the import of such a statement and the effect on a court of the recipient's failure to respond.

Ambiguities versus clear definition

It is easy enough to recognize the really problematical words, such as "may," which should usually be either "will" or "shall."

The party of the second part "may" respond within 30 days.
The party of the second part "will" respond within 30 days.
The party of the second part "shall" respond within 30 days.

Other words, such as "satisfactory," should be clarified by indicating whose satisfaction is necessary to have a job deemed "satisfactory."

> *When the job has been deemed finished in a "satisfactory" manner, the last payment will be made.*
> *When the job has been deemed finished in a "satisfactory" manner **by the architect**, the last payment will be made.*

The more difficult problem is involved with words that appear to be definitive, but which become unclear in the context of a sentence or paragraph.

> *If the job is done well, the client may pay a bonus.*
>
> Does the word "job" require any further definition? What are the specific elements that constitute "the job?" What about "done?" Is the job finished when the roof is on or not until the interior painting has been finished? What about "well?" Some people may consider that the job was done "well." Others may consider it to be quite shabby. What about "bonus?" What amount is to be paid? When?

This should give you an idea of the need for clarity of language at the outset of any business relationship.

What is a contract?

Aside from the definition one might find in *Black's Law Dictionary*, it is fair to say, from a practical standpoint, that a contract is (1) an acknowledged relationship between two or more people (2) with obligations (3) and prerogatives (4) to be exercised and enjoyed under particular terms and conditions. It should have a date at the beginning and should be signed at the end by each of the parties involved.

(1)   "Acknowledged" merely suggests that both parties have agreed to the elements of the contract.

(2)(3) Each party will contribute something (product, services, or money) in return for which that party will be receiving something (product, services, or money). It could be services for money or it could be services for services.

(4)   The terms and conditions usually refer to time elements and the things that need to be done by one party before the other party is obliged to contribute his or her quid pro quo (something in exchange for something else).

The real key to any contract is that each party understands what he or she is expected to do and what he or she is entitled to receive. If you enter a contract and anything is unclear, go back and start again until you understand all of your obligations and prerogatives.

Even the best language (the most carefully designed language) may be subject to ambiguities—especially as a business relationship matures and changes in time. The best protection is to be reasonably careful at the outset to avoid using misleading language or leaving unresolved questions.

Amendments

Although there are simple contracts that require no changes during the course of a contract period, many will. Each party to a contract has expectations that are built into the language of the original document. These expectations may change. Circumstances may cause changes to be made. Anticipated time schedules may have to be aborted. Prices for materials increase. It is true that proper language can anticipate many of these things and assess a cost for each change, depending on circumstance, but the language is often generic—to handle a variety of exigencies—rather than well defined to handle a specific change. A good example is the contract to build a house. How many things will become the cause of contract change due to a change in the price of raw materials, the absence of a subcontractor, inclement weather, or just the client's preference for a different size, shape, or color?

The best way to document these changes is to draft an amendment to the contract that clarifies the time and cost involved. If the contract is a "cost plus" arrangement, the documentation will be merely a calculation. If the contract is based on a negotiated price, then the parties must be willing to negotiate or agree to the more objective opinion of some third party.

Mediation

If two parties have a problem resolving an ambiguity or defending a "cost for change" situation in a contract, the results could be disastrous. Not only might the contract never be completed, but the ensuing litigation would certainly have a long-term negative effect on the relationship of the parties. In addition, their respective reputations in the community will likely never be the same.

A good way to anticipate such problems is to have a clause in the contract that agrees to allow an objective third party to resolve any disagreement. Since such a person who is friend to both parties is rarely waiting for the opportunity to serve in this role, the parties may agree that any such disagreement be taken to an "arbitrator" or a "mediator" instead of the alternative of seeking redress in a court of law. Because of the extensive length of time and the high cost of retaining attorneys and going to court, the "mediator" route has become a very satisfactory method for expediting resolution to these problems in timely and cost-effective fashion.

What is a lease?

Clearly, a purchase is a simple case of paying for a product or service and receiving it. Sometimes payment is made in cash, sometimes in the form of services, sometimes in kind (by another product), or sometimes by a promissory note (which will be discussed later), but the sale is made and each party is finished with all aspects of the sale.

With a lease, one party has the right to use a particular product for a given period of time, during which the other party receives money for extending this privilege. At the end of the lease, the lessor (who owns the property) can take it back. There are also leases with options to buy the product at the end of the leasing period. This means that the lessee (who used the product) has the right to buy it at a particular price (a residual value) or based on a particular formula, such as a percentage of the original price. Make sure you understand the terms and conditions under which you, as the lessee, would have an option to purchase at the end of the lease.

During the lease term, of course, you as the lessee have the obligation to insure and protect the product in anticipation of returning it to the lessor at the end of the lease in the same condition it was in when you started using it. The usual language that follows this "protection" language is "reasonable wear and tear excepted." In other words, it is expected that normal use could result in negative changes to the product. It is the lessee's obligation essentially to protect against "unreasonable or extraordinary" wear and tear. Think of an automobile lease as an example.

The hidden danger of the option

It is always difficult to think in terms of options available at the end of a lease when you are in the throes of negotiating the basic terms at the beginning. Unfortunately, this is the only chance you get to do so. You will certainly want to know if the lease will terminate or expire without any options at all. If it does, you will have to return the equipment (the subject of the lease), and you will have to consider replacement if it was an integral part of your operation. The real questions come up when you do have options.

If you have a buyout clause at the end of the lease, you will need to know if (a) the buyout price is $1.00 (this is sometimes the case when the entire price has been paid during the course of the lease term), or (b) the buyout is based on a specific residual value (this is often the case with automobiles or heavy equipment, when the residual value depends in great part on the mileage or usage put on the equipment during the lease term; the value will remain as quoted providing the usage has not exceeded the anticipated use), or (c) the buyout is based on market value at the time the option to purchase is exercised. (This requires an additional caution since some companies consider the replacement value, some use depreciated value, and still others may predicate the value on the condition of the equipment at the time the option is exercised.)

Don't forget the maintenance contract

Some companies will continue a maintenance contract after you've purchased the equipment. Some will not. This should cause you to wonder about the balance of the equipment's anticipated life and the cost of replacement parts as well as the availability of competent repair personnel. Some companies will continue your maintenance contracts, but watch out for an increase in cost or changes in the contract details. The original maintenance contract may have included all parts and labor. The new maintenance contract may not include labor or parts, or may require the equipment to be shipped to the company's facility. Some may agree to give you a "loaner" during the period needed to repair the equipment. Others may just leave you without the use of the equipment for an open-ended period of time.

The end of the lease

There is a cost of purchasing the equipment when you exercise your option. There may be hundreds or even thousands of dollars to which you might have agreed when you signed the original documents years before. These costs are usually found in the small print on the reverse side of the contract.

If you're running a business you intend to operate for some time, you must actually bifurcate your thinking (separate your thinking into two parts) at the time you negotiate the lease contract. One part should be to negotiate the best deal you can for the term of the lease. The other should be to carefully examine your options at the end of the lease contract.

Then you must factor the options into the lease to see what it is you'll really be paying in the long term as opposed to the cost if you merely financed the purchase of the equipment at the outset. The only problem with this is that many lending institutions might not be interested in loaning you the purchase price based on your particular financial condition at the time you apply for the loan. The manufacturers are obviously a little more liberal in their approach to this problem since it is their job to sell merchandise.

Also, carefully examine the horizon in terms of the level of sophistication of the equipment you are obtaining and the likelihood of a gigantic jump in the level of sophistication that will be available at the end of your lease. One good example is computer hardware and software, which change so dramatically over relatively short periods of time.

A promissory note

In the event you do not have adequate cash to buy a product or service, the provider or vendor may accept your "promise to pay" instead of some or all of the cash required. You might also borrow the money to pay for the product from a third party, like a bank. Then you would have an obligation to repay the money to the person you borrowed from.

In either case, this promise to pay will be evidenced by a paper signed by the borrower (buyer) by which the buyer agrees to pay a certain amount at a particular time (or during a particular period), usually with some additional money (interest) added to it for the privilege of paying later instead of immediately. This paper is called a promissory note. It is also a contract of sorts, so it should have a date at the top, include the terms and conditions of repayment, and be signed by the party to be charged—that is, the party who is promising to pay.

This promissory note, as in any other contract that is clearly defined, is enforceable in a court of law. If it is also witnessed, i.e., the signature is witnessed by an independent third party who can testify that the signature is, in fact, the signature of the borrower, the note is even more secure because the party signing the note is less likely to claim the signature is not his or hers. The strength of this witness is evidenced by the fact that a "witnessed promissory note" in some jurisdictions is enforceable for 20 years. Most notes would be enforceable for a much shorter period of time—normally four years unless the note specifies otherwise.

Be careful, however, to seek the appropriate professional advice before making your own legal judgments. For example, the length of time for potential "enforcement" of the note might be from the date of last payment, not from the date the note was negotiated or signed. Also be careful of language that would destroy the "negotiability" (the ability of the owner of the note—the payee—to sell it to a third party at a discounted rate) of the note in the event you expect to receive a note you might possibly want to negotiate.

The statute of limitations

If one party wants to "sue on a contract," the party must recognize this privilege has certain limitations. Generally speaking, an action can be brought in court within four years from the date of a contract unless the contract otherwise states. Also, remember the witnessed promissory note. This general rule, however, has many exceptions—such as the date of last payment (as noted above), and the waiver by one party not acting in timely fashion—all of which depend on the nature of the agreement and the relationship of the parties. Always seek professional advice whenever these questions arise. Each jurisdiction may have very diverse answers. It is a good idea to examine many of these questions with your professional at the time the document is prepared rather than have to look for the answer after the problem has arisen.

The intimidation factor

Insisting on a written contract for each and every business relationship is not necessarily the best approach to business relationships on a practical level, especially those with a shorter time frame or those involved with smaller financial dynamics. Sometimes it is better to assess your risk and decide that the best approach is an informal one. Sometimes setting out goals in a memorandum simply initialed by the parties to create an acceptable priority list may be the best way to create a document that will survive the memories of the participants. Remember, it is not the malintentioned you are trying to protect against most of the time. It is the failing memory of the parties and the ambiguous language that are more often the core of a problem.

The need for and the nature of a written contract should be dictated by the scope of the activity involved, the length of time for the performance and payment, the intricacies of the terms and conditions, and the amount of money or value involved. You would certainly have a different approach for getting the lawn mowed than you would for having a house built. If you consider these factors on a practical level, you will probably pick the best approach to use in most cases.

The small print

Some people are intimidated by a contract or a lease that has many pages. Although the salesperson would like you to believe that the transaction is a simple one "between friends," the large number of pages seems to belie this casual approach. The fact is that each party seeks to protect those interests that are important to each of them. In a lease—which by its very nature is a long-term relationship—it is certainly necessary that a variety of contingencies be included and defined, primarily for the benefit of the lessor, whose property is going to be at risk.

What is interesting is that most of these contracts, to avoid the negative effect of multiple pages (which the average person would likely take to his or her attorney), are written in type so small that many people can't read it. Sometimes this small print is even put on the reverse side of the signature page, making it appear to be a secondary aspect of the contract. The fact that there are only two pages seems to work to the benefit of the lessor. Most people are told (and they seem to accept it) that the language is "standard" and merely there because it's required by law. *Don't be deceived!*

Two pages might contain the same language that twelve regular size pages would contain. Yes, much of the language is required by law. But don't lose sight of the purpose of the law. The legislature is trying to protect its citizens and has mandated that you be made aware of certain information for your protection. If you don't read it and understand it, woe be unto you. Don't let the small print fool you. Take it to your professional. Have it explained to you. If necessary, make some notes in your own handwriting and in your own language that will cause you to understand and remember the terms and conditions of the contract you are signing. Don't let anyone tell you that it's not really important. If it's not really important, then why is it there?

Although many states now have laws that will allow you to "walk away" from a contract within a certain period of time, it is unfortunate that the reasons normally leading to your change of heart often don't surface until this "rejection period" has past.

Warranties

Many contracts contain certain warranties whereby the purveyor of goods or services guarantees the work or the product for a certain period of time and under a certain set of circumstances. Be careful you understand the parameters—exactly what is covered under the warranty and the conditions under which the coverage is in effect. The roof on a house may be guaranteed, but only for one year. It may include all labor, but not the materials. An automobile can be warranted for 5 years or 50,000 miles, but be careful to note the exclusions, which in some cases may be so extensive as to essentially offer you no protection at all. Read the language carefully. Go over it with your professional if there is anything you don't completely understand or if there appear to be ambiguities that need clarification.

You should not be obliged to sign a contract as it is printed. There is no such thing as a standard contract allowing no change. You may normally negotiate whatever elements are unsatisfactory to you. For an interesting exception to this, see Chapter 7, *Franchise or Otherwise*.

A refresher on corporate signatures

Remember, if you have created a corporation and intend to use its protection, you must sign the contract as an officer of the corporation, not with your personal signature. Be sure to review Chapter 21, *Legal Entities* to be sure you understand the difference.

Key points

- Oral contracts can be legally binding, but much depends on the particular jurisdiction regarding to what constitutes an enforceable agreement.

- Keep narrative notes on all transactions, especially those not covered by a written contract.

- Avoid ambiguities. Don't use language that can be interpreted in more than one way.

- To ensure resolution of any future problems, be sure to put a "mediation clause" in your contracts.

- Go to your professionals whenever you are unsure about your obligations or prerogatives under the terms of a contract or a lease.

Worksheet

- What is the best way to protect yourself if your contract is oral?
- What is the difference between a contract and a lease?
- What does the statute of limitations mean?
- What should you look for under a warranty?
- How do you document changes in a contract?

12

Understanding Your Income Statement

The profit and loss statement

As you examine the basic concept of doing business, you will constantly run across people discussing profit and loss statements, referred to in the vernacular as "P&L's." These are also referred to as income statements. If you are buying a business, you will want to see the seller's P&L. If you are selling a business, you will need to have a P&L you can present to the buyer. If you are operating a business, you will want to develop a P&L to get a "picture" of your business at any given time. Developing P&L's periodically will allow you to compare your business at different times during its development. This will show you where you've been and where you are currently in terms of your short-term and long-term goals. This will give you a better idea as to which of your business decisions have achieved their anticipated goals and which have fallen short. In this way, you should be better prepared to chart your course for the future. See Chapter 3, *The Business Plan* for a more detailed analysis of your business' future based on its past.

The P&L is merely a computation at the end of a given period—a month, a quarter, or a year—that shows the following:

1. **Sales:** This includes the dollars billed for products sold or services performed. It should not normally include the sales tax, since this must be remitted to the government, making your business merely a collection agent on the government's behalf.
2. **Cost of sales** (cost of product): This includes all of the costs attributable to the actual acquisition of raw material or manufacture of your product or the servicing of your equipment.

3. **Gross Profit**: This is merely the difference between "sales" and "cost of sales."

4. **SG&A** (Salaries and general and other administrative expenses): This should include all the additional costs necessary to properly operate the business, including the cost of your facility; monthly payments on your leased equipment (sometimes carried under "cost of sales"—see section on *The danger of statistics*); and payments made on money borrowed for the purchase of equipment, inventory, or the like. (The interest is often found in the P&L, with the principal payments evidenced only by a comparative analysis of the balance sheet—see section on *Balance sheet*.) In other words, SG&A includes every cost of doing business other than the "cost of sales."

5. **Operating Profit**: These dollars represent the profit of the business after deducting all those expenses necessary for the proper operation of the business.

6. **Taxes**: This includes all taxes—including payroll taxes, as well as state and municipal taxes—of every description. Although taxes are carried under SG&A, they are noted here to differentiate them from "sales taxes" mentioned in #1 above.)

7. **Net Profit**: This is the money that you, as the owner, should be able to take to the bank or the grocery store. It is, of course, subject to income tax by the various authorities.

Cash versus accrual

You will hear these two words many times during any discussion of business financial paperwork. They are neither secret concepts nor are they difficult to understand. You should know the difference. A financial picture on a *cash basis* shows all the money actually received and all the money actually spent. A financial picture on an accrual basis shows all the money actually billed, though not necessarily received, and all the money owed (accrued) though not actually paid. It is important to recognize the difference to understand the business picture you are looking at. A good example of the difference will make it clearer.

Each month in a retail outlet, you have to pay rent on the premises from which you do business. At the end of each year, you will have paid rent for 12 months. At least, this is your obligation. This is the rent that will have accrued, whether you actually paid it or not. If you had a bad month in December (in terms of sales and collections) but you had a good month in January, it is possible you might pay the December rent late, perhaps as late as January. You would pay the January rent in January as well. If you looked at a P&L maintained on a cash basis, the previous calendar year would not reflect the full twelve months' rent and the new calendar year would be saddled with an additional month's rent.

Another way of looking at it

Looking at a P&L on an accrual basis, you will find December's rent as an expense during December even though the rent was actually paid in January. On a cash basis, you will find no such rent expense in December (because it wasn't paid in December) and you will find a double rent expense in January. This would make the previous year (which includes December but not December's rent) look better from a profit standpoint (*lesser expenses* would show a *greater profit*) and would make the current year (which does not include December's income but which does include December's rent payment) look worse—*more expenses* for the year, and *less profit*.

It is for this reason that you will normally want to look at a P&L that is created on an accrual basis so you can see how the business actually performed (what the business' obligations actually are) regardless of the way the cash flow of the business might have been manipulated by the owner for purposes other than the actual operation of the business—for example, postponing payment of an obligation until there is money available in the bank to honor the check.

Another aspect of the problem: Jim and Janet Evans

Jim and Janet Evans went to their professional to find out why their business was in financial difficulty. They were keeping their P&L on an accrual basis. At the end of the year, they had sales of $500,000, and all their expenses, which were all paid in timely fashion when they were due, represented about $450,000. Their P&L showed a "profit" of about $50,000 for the year. But they had to borrow money from their bank to pay some personal bills. What was the problem?

Although they had reflected all their sales in their P&L, they had not "collected" all the money that was owed them. In fact, at the end of the year, their receivables—money still owed for services and products sold to their customers—amounted to $75,000. So at the end of the year, even though the P&L showed a profit, their cash position was a loss because *they had paid* all the "accrued" expenses but *they had not collected* all the "accrued receivables."

This is another reason to be examining any business' financial paperwork with an accountant to be sure you understand all the elements and where each fits in the total picture of the business.

Although the P&L, properly prepared, should speak for itself—that is, it has a theoretical integrity of its own—this is not strictly true. You look to the P&L to give you a basic concept of the business' sales, its commensurate expenses, and its ultimate profit. If you do not have an accurate count on either sales collected or expenses paid, you will have something less than an accurate profit picture—in some cases, a good deal less, as the previous example has shown.

The balance sheet

There is also another shortcoming to using a P&L without considering other aspects of your financial paperwork. Looking at a long-term lease, for example, you will want to know what the monthly payments are until the lease ends. Then you will want to decide if you wish to exercise the option to purchase the equipment at a residual or a predetermined cost, trade it in for a new piece of equivalent equipment, or merely throw it out. In some cases, you may have borrowed the money from a bank to pay for the equipment immediately and you will be paying back the loan in incremental, monthly payments. In either case, the accountant may capitalize the actual cost of the equipment and carry the interest to be paid as a separate account. In other words, the interest payments would be found on the P&L as a monthly expense, but the principal payments would only be reflected on the balance sheet. Since a balance sheet is only a picture of the business at a single moment in time, you will need to compare two successive balance sheets to see the dollars actually paid on the principal of the loan or the lease.

A balance sheet for December of 1997 might show a principal balance on the loan of $10,000. The balance sheet for December of 1998 might show a principal balance on the loan of $4,000. This means that you paid $6,000 during the course of the year. If you divide this $6,000 by the twelve months of the year, you can account for the payments made per month: $500 per month. Adding this to the monthly interest payments, you will then have the *total monthly obligation* of that equipment. This will enable you to have an accurate reflection of your actual monthly costs during the year.

See your professional to be sure that you are "finding" these situations and that you have a realistic picture of the business.

What to look for

Being able to understand what the P&L says is the first stage of business financial learning. The second is being able to understand what it means, to interpret what it says, and to "read between the lines."

Although it need not be the first thing you do when analyzing a business, at some point it would be prudent to look at the tax return filed by the individual or the corporation that owns the business. Although it is philosophically appropriate to assume all businesspeople are honest, it is nothing less than good judgment to confirm whatever representations are made about the financial position of a business you may be interested in acquiring. There are many "adjustments" and "juxtapositions" that managers use for various reasons in creating their financial paperwork. It is likely, however, that only justified figures will be submitted to the government for tax purposes. Sales tax returns, for example, will confirm what the business' sales have been. Payroll taxes will confirm employee compensation. Beware the comment by an owner that "the business actually did more than what is reflected on the P&L." If he or she is willing to have something less than an honest reflection of the business on his or her income tax return, what kind of a chance do you think you have of seeing an honest picture relative to other important aspects of the business?

Seasonality, etc.

Providing the business has been in existence long enough, you should examine at least one full year's income statement. Problems of seasonality as well as many other anomalies will only become apparent by comparing one year with another—one June with the previous June, etc. If this history is not available because the business is relatively new, be sure you take a look at industry standards and fluctuations and apply them to the information available to you. See Chapter 14, *How to Research Before Investing*.

Too much dependency

Although it is not to be found in an analysis of the P&L, it's a good idea to check the customer base to see how many big customers are responsible for what percentage of the business. Too much business dependent on too few customers should suggest a potentially dangerous situation. Loss of one of these big customers could be devastating to the business and leave you, as a buyer, with considerably fewer sales than you thought you acquired as part of the business purchase. After noting the statistics, you will be better able to assess the vulnerability of the existing customer base. In some industries, it is also appropriate to note the people who are responsible for the actual sales. Loss of a salesperson who has this kind of control over a substantial portion of the customer base can certainly represent a vulnerability. Be cautious about the stability of the customer base you are purchasing as part of the business. Covenants not to compete—to protect against having salespeople take customers with them to a competitor—are very problematic. Some courts will enforce them; others won't. There are other ways to forestall this problem, including the concept of a deferred compensation plan. See Chapter 8, *Starting a Business or Buying One* and Chapter 20, *Running a Business for Profit*.

Ratios

Many businesses have ratios—such as cost of product in relation to sales—that are consistent industrywide. Others have ratios, such as cost of labor in relation to sales. Although each business must be analyzed on an individual basis, it's a good idea to be aware of these ratios to ensure the particular business is not too far out of line. If it is, there is likely to be a good reason. You should certainly focus on the explanation.

The danger of statistics

There is a positive aspect to examining industry statistics to see if the percentages of any given business appear to be inconsistent with the norm. There is, however, a danger in relying on any such comparative analysis.

To maintain a consistency in handling the financial paperwork for any given business, the accountant will develop a chart of accounts. He or she will allocate a number to each particular category of income and expense. All bills for office supplies, for example, will be under the same number. All health insurance bills will be under a separate number, with liability insurance under yet a different category, with a different number. Each time a check is drawn in payment of a bill, it will have the appropriate number put on it. Each time a bill is received, it will have the appropriate number put on it. In this way, the bookkeeping becomes something less than a nightmare, since all the bills under any given category can be aggregated at any time. It is a good way to be sure that each category contains the correct invoices in the event you are interested in a particular business expenditure. It is also a good way to compare the cost of office supplies for January with the cost of office supplies for June. It might be even more important to see one year as compared to another.

Most businesspeople, together with their accountants, are primarily concerned with the year-end income tax situation. They often don't care what category an expense is carried under. Their primary question is whether it was included as part of the cost of doing business and properly deducted before the profit on which income tax is payable was recognized. In some cases, the accountant may choose to put equipment maintenance under SG&A; a different accountant handling a business in the same industry might create a category for this expense under cost of sales. Sometimes, the designation of the line item makes it difficult to recognize what is included.

Most businesses are broken down into sales, cost of sales, SG&A, and profit. You might be looking at a business and note that its cost of sales appears to be especially low. It might lead you to believe that this business is very well run when you compare this percentage to industry statistics suggesting a considerably higher cost of sales industrywide.

You might, however be terribly deceived. Be sure you understand what is "behind each line item" in the P&L. You must be able to essentially read behind the lines. As the old saying goes, you must be able to compare apples to apples!

Personnel

Longevity of personnel is also a good barometer of the business' stability. If people are employed for long periods of time, it should suggest a good working relationship between labor and management. Also, check the incentives that might be responsible for keeping personnel on board. These could include contracts, profit sharing, pension funds, health insurance, bonus plans, deferred compensation plans, etc. Make sure you understand each of these with respect to each employee and his or her future with the company, as well as your future obligations with respect to any of these emoluments.

Equipment and inventory

What do they have? What do they need? What is on the horizon? How much is still owed on current equipment? What will be needed in the future and what will it cost? By examining these questions, you confront some of the more obvious elements that need definition. How much inventory are you buying? What is the shelf life of the existing inventory from the standpoint of obsolescence, etc.? What is the liquidation value of the inventory if it cannot be sold in the normal course of business?

New equipment needed

The P&L is your best source of information about the finances of a business, if you interpret it properly. But the P&L is only the beginning. The value of a business is usually based—at least in part—on its bottom line profit, and the profit becomes visible only after deducting from the sales all the costs of doing business. If you understand the industry and recognize you need a particular piece of equipment to maintain your competitive position in the marketplace, be especially careful. That piece of equipment may cost you $2,000 a month over the next five years. If sales remain the same and your cost of doing business increases by $2,000 a month—or $24,000 a year—the profit on which the selling price was based will change, and the selling price should change as well.

Remember, you are looking at the cost-to-sales ratio in anticipation of your operating the business after the sale. The fact that the seller didn't invest in the new equipment may be because the seller wanted the higher selling price. If you are obliged to make that equipment purchase immediately after the sale, then you might be seriously overpaying for the business. You will undoubtedly need the necessary dollars on the bottom line to take care of your family and meet the monthly obligations to the seller for the balance of the purchase price. Be sure to read Chapter 18, *How to Value a Business.*

The above is designed to give you a bird's eye view of a business in relation to its financial paperwork. As you can see, a cursory look or a "fair understanding" is hardly good enough. Working with the appropriate professional is the best insurance policy you can buy. Make sure you read Chapter 9, *Dealing with Professionals.*

Key points

- Looking at the P&L is the first order of business in your financial examination of a company.

- Remember that although interest is normally carried on the P&L, principal is often found only in a comparative analysis of the balance sheet.

- Longevity of personnel is a good key to the stability of a business.

- Be careful not to rely too heavily on industry statistics without completely understanding that you must be able to compare apples to apples.

- The need for new equipment immediately after a sale can indicate you overpaid for the business.

Worksheet

- What is the difference between a cash basis and an accrual basis income statement?

- Why is it necessary to look at more than one balance sheet when searching for financial information?

- How can you use the P&L to check on business variables such as seasonality?

- Why is it important to recognize whether a business relies on a small number of big customers for its annual sales?

- What is the danger of comparing a business' percentages with industry-wide statistics?

$\boxed{13}$

Marketing and Advertising

The more understanding you have of the concepts involved in business, the easier it will be for you to maintain control of your business. It is not necessary for you to have an absolute definition for every term used in the marketplace, but it is helpful to understand the differences among terms.

One of these differences is in the application of the words "marketing" and "advertising." Marketing is the general concept of understanding your customer base, your competition and the demographics of your selling geography. Advertising is the method by which you reach your customers with the message about your product or service. These would include such things as brochures, radio and television advertising, billboards and advertising in the various print media.

The totality of your marketplace

Marketing represents the totality of your marketplace as it relates specifically to your particular business. It can, and should, be broken down into a variety of component parts.

You must understand the scope of your potential customer base in terms of geography, how to get your message to them, and how to have them get to you to purchase your product or service. You must recognize the competitive aspect of your product or service; that is, will your product or service uniquely fill a special need, or are there alternatives to the customer doing business with you? What are those alternatives? Are any of them better than yours? Are any less expensive? Is your product or service more or less cost-effective than your competition? It is essential that you maintain a constant marketing surveillance of your business marketplace to be sure you are in a competitive position.

You must also understand the concept of customer alternatives and choice, as well as the reasons behind them. You can, for example, buy a book at a big discount store, but you might be willing to pay more for the convenience of shopping locally. You can certainly buy plants and flowers at a discount store, but you might want the professional advice you get with your purchase at a specialty shop even though the price is higher.

Conventional wisdom

It is easy to understand some of the more obvious marketing concepts. You don't want to be selling bathing suits in Alaska during the winter. You don't want to be selling snowshoes in Hawaii.

The more subtle marketing analyses would suggest that you don't open an expensive jewelry store in a low rent area. However, some seemingly obvious concepts are subject to serious reevaluation. For example, under most circumstances, it would not be prudent to open a business in proximity to and in direct competition with a well established competitor of your particular product or service. On the other hand, many fast food operations insist that their stores with the fastest growth are those that open in a locale in and among other fast food operations. The philosophy is that hungry people drive to areas where there are multiple choices. Then they make their choice.

In the printing business, there was an interesting philosophy in the early sixties. Quick printing was just coming on the scene, and it was thought that opening in the same community with a competitor was smart, because two stores could educate the public more quickly and effectively than one.

So, as you consider your marketplace and particularly your market strategy, be careful to perform a clear analysis before merely accepting what might be termed conventional wisdom in your particular trade or industry.

Discussing these questions with a marketing professional may save you many hours and many dollars, and it may help you avoid many unnecessary mistakes in the long term.

Zeroing in on your customers

If marketing is developing an understanding of your business marketplace, your customer base, and your competitive position, advertising is zeroing in on your customers and bringing your message to them in the most cost-effective manner that generates sales activity.

If you are selling wooden deer for front lawns (see Chapter 1), you will probably advertise (expose your product) by the "show and tell" method. By showing it to your prospective customer, you will usually eliminate any questions about its cosmetics or its utility. Without actually seeing the product, a customer could have many questions about size and intricacy. If you operated the lemonade stand (see earlier chapter) you will probably depend primarily on signage because your location is the key to attracting your audience and your business is not likely to be especially mobile. If you're selling fruit baskets (see Chapter 3), you would probably be most effective with the show and tell method. On the other hand, the items in the basket are easily recognizable, so a brochure with a picture of the product could also be effective.

Levels of sophistication

As you get into more sophisticated products and services, your approach to your customers and exposure of your product or service will become more and more sophisticated. Selling automobiles, for example, is perhaps best done by television commercials, ensuring that you bring the most complete presentation to the largest possible audience. But it is expensive and affords you only a limited time frame.

You might also want to consider some of the new approaches to product advertising recently available as the result of computer technology. Although the Internet requires a somewhat different and more problematic approach in terms of accessing your potential customer, there are some offsetting advantages. Once you have the attention of an interested customer, you will likely have someone who is particularly anxious to examine your product or service in serious detail. After all, they have searched for and found your company. You will then have the opportunity to present a great deal of information within a time frame not afforded by other kinds of media advertising. Consider the advantage of being able to make a sale presentation about an automobile in full color, with sound and movement—and plenty of time. Then consider the fact that you may be able to communicate, one to one, regarding questions, answers and, ultimately, a possible sale.

Cost-effectiveness

It is certainly true that you can, generally, get to more people or deliver a more detailed presentation by spending more money. Business, however, dictates that your advertising dollar must be in proportion to the dollars you generate in sales. The strange paradox however, is that more money spent on advertising does not always mena more profit. If you allocate 10% of sales to an advertising budget, you may find your business with a

10% profit. On the other hand, if you spend 20% for advertising and sales do not increase proportionately, you may end up not generating any additional profit at all.

You must be aware of the amount of sales generated by each advertising dollar and be sure you do enough, without doing too much. It is a delicate balance, to be sure, but one is essential to any business. It requires a constant reevaluation.

Be careful of the worst decision of all. Many businesspeople, when they are having money problems, will "pull-back" on their advertising dollar. Remember that your sales are normally in some ratio to your advertising. Pulling back on advertising may cause sales to drop and end up exacerbating your money problem instead of alleviating it!

Magazines and lists

To achieve cost-effectiveness, you must examine the entire spectrum of your customer base. Then you must decide which is the best advertising approach to deliver your message in the most cost-effective way to the largest segment of potential customers.

In most trades and industries, you will normally find some kind of magazine or newsletter that is distributed to all interested people. This is one way to get to your particular audience without wasting your dollars on those people who do not have an interest in your product or service. Putting an ad in a national non-trade magazine will get to a much larger audience but will be very expensive and will go to many people who may not be part of your customer potential.

Cost per thousand

There may be ways, even in national, non-trade magazines, to zero in on a more targeted audience. Some magazines, for example, cater to women only, some to young professionals, others to new brides, etc. Be careful to examine this myriad of alternatives before you make your advertising commitment. Also, keep in mind that, if you want a test market, you can spend a good deal less money in a newer publication with a smaller audience than with the giants in the field. Advertising dollars are usually calculated on the basis of subscriber numbers or distribution. The term most frequently used is "cost per thousand."

Lists available by category

Another way to advertise in a much more specific way (always depending on the product or service you are selling) is to focus on a very specific audience.

Lists of these specific audiences are available for a price. As an example, if you wanted to reach lawyers, you could get a list of lawyers in a given city. If you wanted only lawyers that practice civil law, as opposed to criminal law, or a list of lawyers that handle only divorce cases, or lawyers that handle auto accidents, you could obtain the list specific to your needs. As you can see, you can zero in on a smaller or more designated group if you choose to do so.

There are lists of people making over $100,000 per year. There are lists of people who own homes. There are lists of those who vote Republican. There are lists of practically every category. You will pay for the list depending on how specific you need it, but in practically every case it will allow you to maximize the effectiveness of your advertising expenditure.

Preparing an ad or a brochure

Preparing an ad for the print media requires an examination of some fundamental advertising principles. You will note that these basics are also quite logical. Be careful not to put "too much copy" (too many words) in your ad. You must "catch" the attention of the reader. You will not normally do this by competing with all the other words on a page. The page becomes a muddle and your ad will get lost. You must put enough space around your printed copy to catch the reader's eye. Remember the advertising axiom, "Once the reader turns the page, you have lost your opportunity to make an impression."

Key words become essential. "Naked" is a word that might get attention. You might not be able to use this word for your particular purposes, so pick one that will get attention and be related in some way to your message.

Naked	Naked	Naked
The naked truth is that we have the best product in town.	*Your bank account won't be naked after shopping with us.*	*Don't let your home be naked to the weather. Use our window protection.*

Print media is based on size and frequency. If you buy a full page in a magazine or newspaper, you might need only one appearance to get your message across and sell your product or service. If you use a one-inch by one-column-wide ad, you may need to depend on many appearances (insertions) to accomplish the purpose of "reaching" and "influencing" the same number of people.

Printing the brochure

If you print a brochure describing your product or service, you will still have to consider "leaving a lot of white space" to make your message easy to read. Be careful of your language—keep it simple. Be careful of your message—keep it simple. Then decide on the size and makeup of the audience you would like to reach. Remember the lists. Remember the costs. Bulk mail to a larger, more general audience may be the same relative cost as first class mail to a shorter, more specific list of potential customers. Which do you think would be best for your business? Would people pay more attention to a letter or a brochure that has a first class stamp on it?

Lisa Lecko

Lisa had her business located near some medical complexes. She decided the medical profession would be a solid customer base for her services. She developed a brochure designed to attract that particular segment of her potential customer audience. After a very successful brochure, she ended up with 35% of her new business coming from the medical community. A specific message was not wasted because it went directly to her potential customer.

Preparing a radio commercial

Just as print media depends on size and frequency, radio depends on frequency and placement. Placement in a newspaper is certainly important: some ads do better on the sports page than they do in the commercial section of the paper. Some financial ads, for example, will do better on the business pages. Similarly, radio is dramatically segmented by audience. Some stations are news oriented, some hard rock, some talk shows. Each has its designated audience. You must decide which is more in tune with your product or service and which age group is likely to be more influenced by your advertising.

There is also time of day to consider. "Drive time," when people are driving to or from work is very effective—and also very expensive. Advertising cost depends in great part on the size of the audience a newspaper, magazine, or radio station can deliver. Many rates, in fact, are conceived in terms like "cost per thousand" readers or listeners.

T.V. advertising is much the same as radio, with the exception that the production costs for preparing the commercials are significantly greater than the dollars necessary to prepare an ad for print or radio commercials. There is also the fact that television stations, for the most part, are more generic in terms of their audience. Radio, remember, is a good deal more specific in terms of the audience to which each station addresses itself.

Other advertising approaches

Then there are promotional activities, like giving away premiums and other incentives, such as rebates and discounts. The list is literally inexhaustible. There are also other incentives, allowing you to expose your product or service to the buying public as well. These include trade shows, participation in sponsorships of such events as sports car racing, and one of the more obvious—the billboard. A good marketing professional can tailor your advertising and promotion needs to your budget as well as to your short-term and long-term goals. Take advantage of them and get "the biggest bang for your buck!"

Bartering

It is quite possible that an advertising medium such as radio might be interested in your particular product or service. A good example is a printing company. You might be able to interest the radio station in a barter situation. You will do a certain amount of printing in return for a certain amount of radio time. Although this is not always possible, it is certainly worth a cursory examination. Can you think of other products that can be bartered or traded for other advertising or marketing products or services?

Key points

- Examining the totality of your marketplace to determine your most cost-effective advertising approach should be high on your priority list.

- The conventional wisdom of one business marketing approach is not necessarily transferable to yours.

- Zeroing in on your customer base is your advertising priority.

- Never lose sight of cost-effectiveness in your attempt to reach your customers.

- Your message must be simple, easy to understand, and to the point.

Worksheet

- When is competition an advantage to your location?

- Why is "show and tell" an effective approach to advertising?

- What is the purpose of using "white space" surrounding your print media ad?

- When is size and frequency considered in advertising?

- Who uses "cost per thousand" as a baseline for advertising rates?

14

How to Research
Before Investing

It is true that—in times of emergency—the entrepreneur will occasionally rely on intuition and instinct to make a quick decision. The majority of successful business judgments, however, are based on careful examination of alternatives. Preparation is the key to good business under all but the most extraordinary circumstances. The most important preparation of all should be the preparation you do before you invest in a business. Most people understand the need for this preparation, but they don't know how to go about starting the exercise.

Looking in the mirror

The first aspect of preparation is to understand a number of things about you, the investor. It is essential that you understand the personal tools necessary to operate a business and to know which of these tools you possess. Perhaps even more important is the other side of that coin. You must understand and acknowledge the tools you don't possess. The best approach to this is to read Chapter 4, *Looking in the Mirror*.

When you've finished this personal assessment of your personal toolbox, you should be ready to make an assessment of your interests and combine this with the goals you hope to achieve and the relationship of your experience and education to the business venture you find most exciting. A good place to start is with Chapter 5, *How Do I Choose My Business?*

Understanding the basics

At this stage, you are probably looking at a particular industry and some aspect of that industry, whether it is in manufacturing or delivering the product or service the industry represents. It is always a good idea to start with a basic history of the industry. It is interesting how much you can learn from an industry's beginnings. It is hardly necessary to examine the basic elements of electricity just because the industry is involved with the use of electricity. However, understanding the real basics of any industry is never a bad idea. If you are thinking of the fast food industry, it would be wise to examine the growth of the industry, and the reasons for the success of one business in relationship to the failure of another. You should ask yourself questions like: Why is one location more successful than another? Why is a diverse menu successful in one area and a simple, basic food item successful in another? What is the relationship of size to success in different areas? What about traffic patterns? What about competition? Will you have to deal with unions? What about the incidence of personnel turnover and the resulting need for constant training and supervision? This is just touching the surface of the question. As you can see, examining an industry is no small problem. But there are some ways this exercise can be simplified.

Manufacturers, vendors, and the trade magazines

Every industry has equipment or inventory that is used in the entrepreneurial operation. The salespeople involved in selling these products are probably as knowledgeable as anyone else in terms of the history of the industry, its current patterns of development, and what is anticipated in terms of changes in the methods of doing business. The danger of this information is obvious. These people will invariably be looking at the industry through rose colored glasses. After all, their livelihoods depend on their sales, and their sales depend on an optimistic look at the future. On the other hand, this is a good place to start because it will probably reinforce your optimism about the future of the industry. It will certainly make you more knowledgeable with respect to the basic elements on which the industry is based. It should also give you the names of the appropriate trade magazines, and help you formulate questions to ask of people already in the business.

The trade magazines are usually loaded with information about equipment and products, as well as all the additional items that are collateral to the industry but important in the day-to-day activities of those operations that sell and distribute the products. In addition to product advertising, most trade magazines also publish articles by both outsiders and insiders discussing various aspects of the business. This information should generate additional questions. Remember, it's knowing what questions to ask that is the key to your investigation.

These magazines, as well as web sites affiliated with the industry, will often have statistics available for you to examine. These statistics will likely provide you with information about the most dynamic successes in the industry, the number of businesses that have exceeded certain sales figures, the number of personnel necessary to achieve these figures, the type and amount of equipment necessary to maintain these levels of sales, the latest consumer statistics on need or preference, and budgets that must be maintained to move from one sales plateau to another. Each industry has its own standards of statistical evaluations, some depending on general geographical locations, some predicated on size of operations. The real question is, To what extent are the statistics valuable in terms of your particular industry? If you are buying an existing business, the statistics will likely be less valuable. If you are starting a business from scratch, the statistics should be of considerably greater value. Be sure you read Chapter 8, *Starting a Business versus Buying One.*

The franchise decision

Although you may not be interested in buying a franchise—either an existing location or a new location—the franchise is an excellent place to find out a lot about any given industry. Every franchise, in every state, by law, must make available to any buyer candidate a disclosure document. This disclosure is designed to inform any buyer about the industry, its history, and how it functions as well as some specifics about the particular franchise company. Although most franchise companies do not give these disclosures to anyone other than a serious buyer, they are normally available either through the company or—in the event you are considering the purchase of an existing franchise—through the franchise owner. Since so many businesses concepts in the American marketplace have been franchised, it is very likely the industry you are looking at will be represented. Although the information in the average disclosure is usually pertinent to the particular franchise company, the generic information will invariably be very valuable and, as always, will probably suggest more questions to help you in your continuing examination of the marketplace and the part that the particular industry plays in that marketplace.

Ask the person who owns one

There is no better way to research a business or validate your findings from previous examinations than to discuss the day-to-day business activity with someone who experiences it every day. There are some businesses that may not be susceptible to such scrutiny. There are those new ideas that have no equal in the marketplace and there are variations on existing products or services for which a comparative analysis would be helpful, but not definitive. For the most part, however, you should be able to find a comparable situation, the experience of which can be used to answer at least some of your questions.

Keep in mind that the internal operation of the business may be easier to analyze because every similar operation functions in pretty much the same way. It is not so much the similarities you need to examine, but rather the differences.

If the operation is a franchise, you'll want to get as much information as possible about the relationship between the franchise company and the franchise owners. You particularly want to find out about their training program, their ongoing support, and the costs of each. For a thorough discussion of this, be sure to read Chapter 7, *Franchise or Otherwise*.

You will want to see how the customer audience is converted to a consumer group. You will want to know what kind of advertising is being used to make this happen. You should review Chapter 13, *Marketing and Advertising* to get a clearer picture of what is being done relative to what ought to be done and the cost factors involved.

If the owner of the business you're examining has developed a business plan that has been the road map of the business, it would be terribly helpful if the owner would share this with you. You will be able to see what the business plans were, how much money was allocated for growth, and to what extent success has been achieved. You will want to review Chapter 3, *The Business Plan* as you embark on this aspect of your investigation.

Taking the boss to lunch

It is very interesting that most successful entrepreneurs are delighted to share most of their information with you, providing that they are satisfied you are in earnest and that you do not intend to become a direct competitor. This is one reason to approach the owner with some degree of care and a great degree of sincerity. In some cases, the owner may even be inclined to disclose more personal and significant information with you, such as the business' income statement. If you should get this lucky, be sure you familiarize yourself with Chapter 12, *Understanding Your Income Statement* to take advantage of these numbers being made available to you. Remember the all-important cost-to-sales ratio. Be sure you treat these entrepreneurs with the respect they deserve: pick up the check if you are lucky enough to have some of their personal time by taking them out to dinner or lunch.

The more subtle elements

Location

As you speak with someone already in the business—and this should become a very high priority, if not the highest priority, in your investigation process—you will eventually reach a point where your general knowledge of the industry and of the particular business operation becomes reasonably good. You must now concentrate on those aspects of the operation that may change as you open your particular business in a different location. Location, indeed, is one of the most appropriate questions. You certainly can't duplicate the location—after all, there is only one corner of 5th and Market. By examining the features of the 5th and Market location, however, you may be able to apply those "features" to a similar location in your own neighborhood or city. Keep in mind such things as traffic patterns, the ability to make a left turn, islands that force traffic in particular directions, visibility of signage, allowability of signage—including municipal regulations as well as landowner preferences for consistency—and, particularly, parking availability for those businesses where this is an important element for the convenience of the customer.

Personnel

Another of the more subtle elements is the question of personnel. To what extent will you be dependent on key people? Who are these people? How much do they get paid? What is their relationship to the customer? How vulnerable is the business in the event they choose to leave? Be careful of the salesperson problem mentioned in a previous chapter. What is the availability of people with similar expertise in your local marketplace? In other words, how easy or difficult would it be to replace these people, and to what extent would their absence create problems for the business?

You'll want to analyze the number of personnel required to achieve and maintain a particular sales volume. Depending on the kind of business you're looking at, you'll want to examine certain other aspects of the personnel question, such as cross training, time flexibility, and outsourcing. An experienced entrepreneur will be able to give you solid reasons for maintaining certain aspects of the business internally and turning to outsourcing for others.

To give you some idea as to what kind of a relationship you might want to create between yourself and your employees, you might inquire as to which if any employees are under contract and what the terms and conditions of those contracts are. You might also ask if the employer has any deferred compensation plans to protect against the loss of a key employee and the potential loss of customers as a result. There is also the question of what amenities, if any, are offered to the employees, such as health insurance and pension or profit sharing plans. Keep in mind that each industry has its standards, and even the standards are usually only guidelines. They are not mandated. Also, remember, the better informed you are, the more likely you will do the right thing.

The role of the professional

Professionals can include lawyers, accountants, and consultants, as well as experts in a particular industry or with a particular experience. The latter category might include people in the food industry with special food procurement experience or people in the computer industry with specialized software expertise. Although certain businesses might suggest you seek out a particular professional at a particular time, it is rarely too early to do so.

Even the professional—the lawyer, for example—often seeks expert advice *before* he or she decides to take a client's case. With the complexities of the modern day marketplace and the proliferation of malpractice actions against lawyers, the competent lawyer usually prefers to understand the nuances of a case before taking on the responsibility of legal representation. Do you think a similar philosophy should prevail before you take on the responsibilities of a new business?

The money you spend on professional advice in the early stages of your investigation will invariably save you dollars in the long term. Keep in mind that a professional needs to understand your goals and aspirations, and needs to know about your available capital and potential partners or joint venture participants. This professional will be in a better position to advise you along the way than someone who is brought into the picture midstream and asked for a decision based on too little information. See Chapter 9, *Dealing with Professionals* for a clear perspective on this.

The big mistake

A new entrepreneur is not likely to be expert in the basic operations of any business. Nor is he or she likely to fully understand the income figures of the business in terms of the cost-to-sales ratio concept. Yet the average entrepreneur does not like admitting how little he or she knows. *This is a big mistake!*

There is no point in going through even the most exhaustive investigative analysis if you are not going to completely understand the nature and implications of the information. When it comes time to examine income statements, you should take your preliminary look with an accountant to be sure you understand the basics. In addition, just looking at the income statement is rarely enough. You must be able to understand what each line item represents to get a real feeling for the cost-to-sales ratio, to say the least. If a cost item is a nonrecurring expense, you should recognize that this will not represent an ongoing cost to you after the sale. If a line item represents a lease of equipment with an option to buy, you'd better find out what the residual value is for acquisition purposes. It may be $1.00 or it may be many thousands of dollars. Don't allow yourself to be misled because you are too embarrassed to acknowledge how little you know.

Reflect on Chapter 11, *Contracts and Leases*, especially the question of "options to renew." Make sure your attorney explains this to you clearly and in language you can understand, or you may be making important decisions about your future based on misinformation or lack of adequate information. Remember, litigation to resolve ambiguities, *after the fact,* can be time consuming and expensive—a bad way to run a business.

Working at it before you buy it

Depending on a variety of personal factors, there is another way to investigate your business opportunity. Work at it before you buy it. This opportunity does not always present itself. In some cases, there is insufficient time or money to afford this luxury. In other situations, the opportunity to purchase or start a business or join others in the adventure might not allow the time for such a situation. There is also another negative aspect to this kind of early participation. You may learn some basics about a particular aspect of the business—your job—but never get a complete picture of how the pieces come together to form the whole. In addition, most employers are not expecting to run a school or a training course for potential competitors. Many sellers are not anxious to have a potential buyer working for the business only to leave and open his or her own business in competition. Be careful to avoid such problems. It can create long-term problems. If you choose this route to investigate the business and the industry, be careful not to fall into the category of those who "can't see the forest for the trees." Looking at a tree will not give you an adequate idea of what the forest looks like. You will not necessarily see the owner agonizing over long-term business problems if you only get to understand one or two pieces of equipment.

Be careful of overkill:
(Don't become a researcher instead of an entrepreneur)

As anxious as the average entrepreneur candidate is to get started, there are many who don't know when to stop investigating and start investing. Certainly, a lack of investigating or an investigation that does not go into sufficient depth is a mistake. The opposite to this, however, must be respected as well. It is easy enough to examine any business to the point where the diamond loses its lustre. There is also the possibility you may encounter so many negatives from various sources that you will second guess your original judgment. In some cases, this is exactly the kind of information you need to prevent you from making a bad investment. In others, you may be needlessly prevented from fulfilling a life's dream. Be careful in both instances. Be careful also of becoming a researcher instead of becoming an entrepreneur. You can't learn to swim without going into the water. And you can't become a champion until you've mastered the strokes.

Don't be afraid to take the chance. Follow the rules, the suggestions, and your own game plan. Achieve the goal. Enjoy the success. And remember what failure is really all about.

Failure is not the entire journey. It is merely a stop on the journey. Make it a short stop—and move on. The brass ring is there but you must reach out to get it. You can ride the merry-go-round and look at it every time you pass it. Or you can reach for it after you've made an assessment of the odds and the problems. What are you going to do?

Key points

- Get your most optimistic information from the manufacturers and vendors selling equipment and products in the industry.
- Examine the trade magazines for collateral items and articles about the industry.
- Be careful how you use statistics to your advantage.
- Franchise disclosures represent a good source of information.
- Work closely with your professionals at an early stage.

Worksheet

- Why is it important to check your own personal toolbox?
- What is the problem of relying on information from manufacturers and vendors?
- Are statistics more important when you buy a business or when you start a new one?
- Why is it difficult to work in an industry before you buy into it?
- What is your best source of information?

15

Taking Over
a Family Business

[Authors Note: Since the greatest vulnerability in a family takeover is to the parent, this chapter is written primarily from the parent's perspective. Recognizing the family dynamics will represent the new owner's best preparation.]

It shouldn't surprise anyone contemplating such a "takeover" that the title might more appropriately be, ***Preparing to Turn Over Your Family Business.*** Preparation is the key to the success of the transition and the ultimate survival of the business.

In some cases, the two generations have been working together in the business before the concept of "takeover" entered the picture. This is not always the case, however. In today's current business marketplace, an existing business, started by a parent, offers a unique job opportunity to a son or daughter, as well as a potential for the future. With the limitations of job availability and the competitive element being as strong a market force as it is, many young people are looking at the family business for the first time with a new perspective.

Another aspect of this is that, in many cases, the parents are trying to perpetuate the business for their own benefit—their retirement. Leaving the business in the hands of "family" might be a more secure transition than taking a chance by selling the business to a stranger, even with a lesser down payment or, in some cases, no down payment.

The relationship before the takeover

There are many variables in terms of the relationship that exists just prior to a family takeover. In some cases, your son or daughter may have been working in the business for such a long period of time that he or she has actually become an integral part of the business' operation. In other cases—and acknowledging this is sometimes difficult to admit—your son or daughter may never have become an integral or necessary part of the operation, regardless of how long he or she may have been associated with the business.

With respect to a working relationship that already exists, some parents never think the children are capable regardless of how hard they may try and how effective they might appear to their peers. There are other parents who give their children credit for total competence without ever having done a really objective analysis of their performance. Other variations include having a good general manager who is not a member of the family and who is perfectly competent to maintain the continuity of the business. Is he or she capable of getting along with your son or daughter in your absence even though the surface relationship appears to be working well when you are present? On the other hand, if you have such a general manager and you give the operating responsibility to your son or daughter, will you lose the general manager and, in turn, jeopardize the continuity of the business, particularly as you will no longer be available for day-to-day consultation?

In one situation, the owner of a business had both his son and daughter working in the business with him when he succumbed to a heart attack. Neither of his children had any intention of making the business a permanent part of his or her future. The business, however, represented so large a portion of the father's estate that both children agreed to maintain the continuity of the business for the sake of their mother. The problem of holding the pieces together during the takeover period—for which no preparation had been made—caused tremendous pressures between the children.

The daughter finally left. The son was not capable of handling a lot of the paperwork by himself. He was neither trained for this responsibility nor did he have the inclination to handle the myriad details, which had normally fallen on the shoulders of his sister. The business eventually got into trouble. It survives today, but its business tempo will never be as dynamic as it was during the father's tenure. Adequate preparation could have avoided many, if not most, of the problems faced after the father's death.

Facing a harsh reality—stale signatures

The extent to which you will want to maintain a relationship with the business after takeover depends on a variety of things. To what extent is the continuity of the business essential to your retirement? To what extent are you still responsible for certain contractual obligations, like the lease, even though you are no longer connected with the operation of the business? Keep in mind that when you signed the lease, it may have been for five years or it may have been a five-year lease with successive five-year options. If it was such a lease, you are still responsible for payment even though you may not have been involved with the business for many years. You wouldn't be the first person to whom this harsh reality came as a surprise after leaving the business.

Day-to-day consultation after takeover

Are you ready to give up the business and its equity by telling your son and daughter that it is a "sink or swim" situation? To what extent are you obliged to make working capital available in the event the business enters a slow period or the industry takes a downturn? In other words, just how quickly are you prepared to cut the cord?

There are a number of things to keep in mind. Primarily, there is the question of the business concept. You have undoubtedly formed the business and maintained it with a certain philosophy and with the idea in mind that it take a certain position, or niche, in the particular trade or industry of which it is a part. It is very easy for someone to quickly and dynamically superimpose a whole new set of principles on the business in your absence. Some of these may be only subtle changes with little long-term effect; others may well impact the very nature of the business.

Cost-to-sales ratios

It is a good idea to monitor the business by maintaining a certain cost-to-sales ratio. You can mandate, for example, that until you, the seller, have been paid in full, the buyer shall not allow the labor factor (including his or her income) to exceed a certain percentage of sales. By doing this, it would be difficult for the new owner to dramatically change the business concept without seeking some agreement from you. Another protective device is to require your approval on any business purchase in excess of a certain dollar amount. After all, you must protect against the buyer "using" the cash flow to pay everything and everybody to the exclusion of you, the seller.

Staying in touch versus staying in control

Here is a place to take care. On the one hand, staying the course and maintaining continuity are important. On the other hand, you must never lose sight of the creative juices of new blood and new energy. You must recognize that the business marketplace is a constantly changing environment. It is one that feeds on creativity and change. It is one where the competitive element can be quickly lost by not taking advantage of change when change is necessary or appropriate. It is for this reason that you should stay in touch. This does not mean "stay in charge." It means "stay in touch." Make sure you can monitor the changes and recognize the impact each change will likely have on your position in the marketplace, before it is too late to remedy. After all, larger companies do this by having a board of directors.

In a certain situation, the son took over the business after spending many years as an apprentice under the supervision of his father. Immediately after takeover, in an attempt to ensure a good competitive position, he leased some new "state-of-the-art" equipment.

The increase in his productivity was minimal. The increase in his client base was also small. But the increase in monthly obligations was substantial. He had not generated the advertising necessary to "fill the time" of the new equipment and make the lease—and the monthly payment—worthwhile. The father would have taken a much more conservative position. He would have carefully examined the market potential before making the investment. The father was devastated, but the paperwork was already signed. The modest retirement income the father had hoped for turned into a Chapter 7 bankruptcy. Father, instead of retirement, got a new job. Staying "in touch" after the takeover would undoubtedly have netted a different result.

Vulnerability of assets after takeover

Unfortunately, when you start a business, you sign a long-term lease for the premises; you sign a franchise agreement for ten or twenty years; you sign leases or contracts for the use or purchase of equipment; and, indeed, you might very well sign a promissory note for money borrowed from a bank or lending institution, or from the seller from whom you purchased the business. These people might be very encouraging, from a personal standpoint, when you tell them you are turning the business over to your son or daughter. Normally, however, they will not be inclined to release you from your obligation, because you are probably more stable in the community and likely have more assets than your son or daughter. In other words, your assets and your dollars will remain at risk even though you may no longer be personally involved in the business.

Remember, even though you may have a corporation that is responsible for most of those obligations, you have probably signed all the paperwork as an individual as well. Most banks, landlords, and purveyors of expensive equipment will not allow the corporate signature without either a cosigner or a guarantor. In either case, you will remain responsible until the entire debt is paid. The reason for this is that most closely held corporations, particularly new ones, are not substantially funded. Having access to a limited reservoir of dollars is no comfort to the purveyor of expensive equipment or the holder of a long-term lease, the aggregate amount of which can be quite substantial.

In one situation, a son, who was especially knowledgeable in a particular business, took over from his mother and father. He operated the business very well for a number of years. In fact, he grew the business quite dramatically. Then he hit a downturn and the business verged on the edge of disaster. The franchise company, the landlord, and the equipment companies all came after the mother and father, neither of whom was capable any longer of operating the business. They weren't even aware of the business' day-to-day activity; but their assets were still vulnerable. This business has made all kinds of arrangements for readjusting its debts, and will probably survive. In this case of a permanent takeover, arrangements should have been made to close out certain obligations after a given time period and let "the folks" off the hook, providing the business showed proper stability in the early stages, which it did.

Moving your business into the hands of the next generation is a dream held by many parents. The children recognize the great opportunity that such a transition provides. It is unfortunate that, in the face of this joy, there are pitfalls to which little or no serious consideration is given—until it is too late. If you are involved in such a situation, make sure the very nature of the business, its position in the marketplace, and its future in the competitive field are completely understood. Make sure a plan for the future and a pattern for its potential growth are studied and understood by all parties involved.

Make sure that certain investments, particularly in the early days, are discussed, analyzed, and agreed on rather than allowing individual, inexperienced judgments to prevail. *It is in the nature of youth to reach out creatively toward the future. It is in the nature of parents to reflect on the past to ensure a conservative approach for the future. Neither is wrong. It is, in fact, in the combination of these things that you will find the most successful transitions.* It is worthwhile to take the time for this exercise.

Uncle Sam as your new partner—after the sale

Because of the tax implications of every sale transaction, it would be careless of you not to consider the methods by which you can eliminate—or at least minimize—the taxes that might be payable upon the transfer of your business by family members. The nature of the tax structure in this country allows for a variety of ways to approach this problem. These alternatives range from creating a particular legal entity, which will allow incremental increase of ownership over a period of time, to giving participation to the family member on a gift basis—being sure not to incur a gift tax in the process—to the holding of the stock by a trust or the use of a family limited partnership. Along with most of these alternatives, it will be critical to create an insurance program that will handle the tax problem by making dollars available for the purpose of acquiring stock without diluting its value or the participation of ownership. Failure to do so will often defeat the intention of the original owner.

A brief analysis of some of these alternatives suggests that a gift, like an irrevocable trust, can be inappropriate because it may cause the owner to lose active control of the enterprise during his or her continuing operation of the company. This is not usually the goal the owner seeks to achieve. The limited partnership concept, on the contrary, allows the owner, the general partner, to maintain control while having portions of the "equity ownership" in the hands of limited partners. Remember that the limited partners are neither obliged nor permitted to participate in the day-to-day activities of the business. If they do participate, they may find themselves in a "general partnership" status, having lost the protection of the limited partnership concept. What this can mean is that, instead of merely losing the investment they made, they may find themselves responsible for all the business debts (see Chapter 21, *Legal Entities* for a more extensive examination of this question).

Resolving ambiguities

In a somewhat unique situation, an owner of two separate businesses had his son operating one of them and his daughter operating the other. As good fortune would have it, both locations were dynamically successful. It is true that the owner had not only initiated both businesses, he had also been responsible for training his children and, indeed, had trained them well. For the first ten years, he had been a "hands on" operator. In more recent times, he had kept a particularly watchful eye on the businesses and scrutinized the purchase of equipment and the hiring of personnel.

In one case, his daughter owned 25% of the operation. This paperwork had been initiated early on at the daughter's request. In the other case, however, the owner's son did not have the same foresight. He had not made arrangements for a legal transfer of any kind and, as a result, had no equity participation at all.

Although it is accepted practice that business agreements be memorialized in writing, this same philosophy oftentimes seems not to prevail in the family environment. In this case of father and son, the father had been sharing 25% of the profits of the business with his son for the ten years the son operated the business—even to the extent that he legally did it in "gift form," which allowed the son to avoid the payment of taxes on these dollars.

When the time came for the son to "buy" the business, he expected to pay only 75% of the purchase price (as did his sister) because he felt that he already owned 25%. In fact, he didn't *own* 25%—it was never agreed to and never put in writing. Resolving this ambiguity almost led to a family feud and a failure of the ownership transition.

Interestingly, the matter was resolved by a third party's intervention. Both parties were asked to adjust their expectations in favor of maintaining the family relationship and avoiding a family disaster. The son agreed to "buy" the 25% he felt he owned. In turn, the father agreed to base the price for the 25% on the value of the business as of the time the son took over, some 10 years earlier—rather than at the current value, which was much greater and which was, in great part, attributable to the energy and work of the son during that period. This compromise solution saved everybody's pride and allowed the family to remain intact.

Don't let the family relationship create ambiguities. They can be devastating. Treat the family "business" as a true business relationship and prevent such ambiguities from undermining the family.

Letting go of the controls and protecting the future

The last critical element that ought to be factored in is the fact that both children had been involved in their respective operations for ten years and both were in their early forties. They wanted autonomy and ownership, both of which had been promised but not delivered. They were now threatening, subtly or otherwise, that without a buyout situation, each might leave his and her respective positions. The owner's problem was his inability to completely turn over the responsibility of each operation. He still felt that neither was mature enough to make the hard choices in terms of purchasing equipment and selecting the most appropriate road for the future of the business. This is not an atypical situation between parents and their children. Certainly, it is true that each operation might change to some degree without the original owner's ongoing supervision, but this would likely be the case no matter who bought the business. In this case, however, the father's choices were becoming clear and time was becoming critical.

Each business had a fair market value of about $500,000 if the businesses were sold to a third party. Without the son and daughter at the helm of each business, however, it was conjectural whether the successes would be maintained, because personal service is a key in this particular industry. In addition, in the event of an unsuccessful takeover by a stranger, it would not be possible for the original owner to return to active participation in the businesses. Unless a sale in each case was orchestrated with present operating personnel intact, the positive selling values of the businesses could be undermined.

What would your decision be? Selling a business at the right time is often critical. The danger of turning total responsibility over to another person is part of the selling—and part of the risk. A simple assessment of the above situation would lead to a single conclusion. The failure to sell could destroy the retirement income that had been the owner's dream for years. Remember, putting some protective devices in the agreement between the parties, such as "maintaining ratios," is perfectly normal in any sale, family involvement notwithstanding (see Chapter 18, *How to Value a Business*).

This brief examination should make it clear that any approach to the tax questions and the owner's ability to maintain control during his or her lifetime—as well as all the particular aspects of transfer and turnover—will require advice from the experts. You should consult the team of your attorney, your accountant, your business consultant, and your insurance planner before you contemplate any definitive move.

Key points

- Keep in mind that a long-term lease has long-term consequences.
- Staying in touch is not the same thing as staying in charge.
- Maintaining the original course of a business combined with necessary and appropriate changes in new direction is the predicate for continuing success.
- The tax implications of family succession should be a high priority concern.
- Maintaining control during the transition years must be carefully orchestrated.

Worksheet

- What makes "maintaining ratios" a good method for avoiding precipitous changes in the direction of a business during takeover?
- Why will most manufacturers and vendors require a personal signature on a corporate purchase?
- Why is it a good idea to consult an insurance planner when thinking about family succession?
- How does a limited partnership preclude interference by the investors?
- How can you protect against the risk of turning over a business to someone who might want to make significant changes in the business?

16

Improving Your Business

It is true that each business has its own operational peculiarities. One business may be inventory heavy. Another may create and deliver product using expensive equipment. Aside from this kind of exception, most businesses follow a pretty basic format in terms of operation.

The pie chart

The average business will have four basic parts, equivalent to four pieces of a pie. These parts can normally be addressed as: 1) sales, 2) cost of product, 3) salaries and general and administrative expenses (SG&A), and 4) profit.

1. *Sales* usually represents all gross revenues excluding sales tax.
2. *Cost of product* is a basic whether a business is in retail, buying inventory for sale, or in manufacturing, buying raw material for production or assembly.
3. *Salaries* and *General Administrative Expenses:*
   a. *Salaries* (cost of labor) is even simpler. This cost involves people. Whether they are internal to an organization or an outsourced capability, whether they are behind a piece of equipment or dealing directly with the customer, people will always be an integral aspect of a business and a necessary cost factor.
   b. *General administrative expenses* encompass all other expenses of doing business and will include rent, electricity, telephone, repair and maintenance of both

premises and equipment, insurance, gas and oil, and advertising. (This list is not exhaustive.)

4. *Profit* is the money from all sales that is "left over" after the payment of cost of labor, cost of product, and all salaries and general and administrative expenses.

The concept of improving your profit is normally a question of either increasing sales or decreasing expenses. Neither course is necessarily simple.

Increasing sales

Increasing sales usually means one of two things. You must either increase your customer base or increase the amount of goods or services currently being purchased by your existing customers. In either case, you will need to spend money. This will certainly increase either your administrative expenses or your cost of labor.

You will either need additional personnel to sell the product or service or you will need to spend advertising dollars to expose the product or service to your new or existing customer base.

The problem is that the expenditure for product exposure will normally precede the increase in sales. You will therefore have to have money available—working capital—to make this investment in advertising. If you don't, your growth potential may not be realized. For an explanation of this sequential problem, see Chapter 1, *The Financial Picture*. For the source of such funding, see Chapter 10, *More on Investors and Partners*.

A unique approach—with two big mistakes

Mary Burnham came back to her business after being away due to a number of out of state family problems. The manager, whom she left in charge, did not take her responsibilities seriously and the business suffered. Jobs were not being handled with attention to quality and, in Mary's absence, the customer base had grown smaller.

She attended to this problem in a manner she thought would put her back in the ball game. She made two serious financial mistakes, however. The first was that she approached a number of substantial accounts with the proposition that, if they moved their business to her shop, she would give them a lot of preliminary work at no cost. Giving away this "preliminary work" was essentially giving away the entire profit on each job. The second mistake was that she took their business without the *usual* precautions of checking their references to ensure they were good payers. Many were not!

Mary not only lost money on the jobs she took, she was not able to collect money from many of them. After taking advantage of her "proposition," many of the accounts went to other competitors in the marketplace for their ongoing business. Mary went out of business!

These customers obviously "used" Mary's proposition to their advantage and then returned to the competitors to whom they normally gave their business.

Do you think they thought Mary less than professional because she was "discounting" to an extreme degree? Do you think they took advantage of her "proposition"—and then left—because they felt she was probably on the verge of going out of business? Do you think businesspeople are actually so selfish and malintentioned in the business marketplace? What would you have done?

Too much confidence, too little reality

Donna Sharon was a woman with confidence. For 15 years, she had proven herself more than adequate to the task in a corporate bureaucracy. She was sales oriented, paid attention to detail, and understood the basics of financial paperwork. She decided to convert these corporate talents to serve the goal of building a personal business—becoming an entrepreneur. She had the emotional backing of her family and she pursued her industry investigation with the same vigor that had been the predicate for her success in the corporate world.

She found an industry she liked, one in which her aggressive sales experience would be a positive factor. She examined some businesses in that industry and picked the one she wanted. She used two criteria to make her business choice. She picked a business that was "barely making it," a business just about "breaking even," a business that did not show any profit to speak of. The sellers explained that they were not sales oriented people, as a result of which they had not really enjoyed the maximum customer potential the area offered. Although the equipment in the business was something short of industry standards as well, the price of the business was less than that of competitive operations although more than it was worth. Donna's attitude was that this was an opportunity to take over a business that had growth potential as yet untapped.

The second criterion was that the price, although inflated from the standpoint of any objective analysis, required less cash than comparable operations. The bulk of the purchase price would be paid on a promissory note over ten years. Clearly, with an appropriate increase in sales (of which Donna was completely confident), the payments on the note, as well as the income she personally expected to earn, would not be problematical.

Donna was wrong! The reasons are clear. The investment turned out to be her worst nightmare.

Since Donna expected to handle the "outside sales," the seller agreed to stay with the business and handle the internal operations. *The seller received an ongoing income. Donna took nothing from the business for the two years she owned the business.* She did build sales, but not to the extent she anticipated. In addition, much of the business she was able to generate she was unable to fulfill because of the obsolete nature of the equipment. She barely managed to maintain the expenses necessary to operate the business and meet the payment schedule on her note to the seller for the balance of the purchase price. Her self-esteem took a big hit, her husband's emotional backing became somewhat soft, and her physical health began to suffer, leading to doctors and prescription medicine. She put the business up for sale.

Even with the increased sales, the purchase price was barely sufficient to meet the outstanding debt to the original sellers, who were not interested in making any concessions. Donna finally managed to sell the business to her key employee. She lost her original investment. She lost her self-confidence. She lost her dreams.

A business must be able to pay for itself! The seller is entitled to convert the earned equity of the business to a purchase price—not the anticipated efforts of the buyer. These efforts should convert to the buyer's income!

Donna was an excellent buyer candidate. Although she had limited cash for investment, she had substantial assets, a strong track record as a businessperson, and the appropriate background and experience to handle the business. The fact is that most sellers would have been happy to take less cash up front and to have the security of her assets (and her husband's assets—which is one reason she couldn't even file a bankruptcy) and her potential to maintain the continuity of the business. With a bigger business, the existing cash flow might have been able to handle all the costs and expenses of the business, including Donna's salary. This would have allowed Donna to build the business and use the "new profit" to buy the equipment necessary to fulfill the business' increased requirements.

Increasing capability

Increasing capability is another way of increasing profit, but you still face the "chicken-or-the-egg" problem. To produce a better product, or to produce the same product in a shorter period of time or at a lesser cost, you may need to augment the equipment you are currently using or buy equipment to replace any that may be obsolete. Although either of these cost factors may increase your efficiency and, in turn, your profit, you will need the money to buy the equipment before you will be able to enjoy the increased sales and profit.

Buying versus leasing

The manufacturers of this equipment recognize the chicken/egg syndrome and are anxious for you to acquire their equipment. The marketplace has developed a method by which you can acquire the equipment and pay for it from increased sales. This is what is known as your leasing alternative. Be sure to read Chapter 11, *Contracts and Leases.*

Improving your business

By taking advantage of the leasing alternative, many businesses can use new equipment without needing to pay the entire price up front. This allows the business to grow with minimal cash availability. In most cases, you will need to have good credit to do this, and the seller will normally take a security interest in the equipment until it's fully paid for. In the event you fail to make the payments, the seller has the right to take the equipment back. You will then have lost the lease payments already made and no longer have the equipment available to you. In some cases, even though the equipment has been repossessed, you may still be responsible for the balance of the payments due under the leasing contract.

This caution is mentioned because you must make some very careful judgments before you allow your business to take on the responsibility of these lease payments. You must be able to assure yourself that, with either current sales or with the anticipated sales, you will definitely be able to meet the lease payment schedule. Failure to do so can lead to unexpected circumstances, the worst of which would be the destruction of your entire business.

Salespeople

Even the hiring of salespeople represents the same chicken/egg problem. Salespeople need to have an immediate income when they start working. It is true, however, in practically all fields of endeavor, that the efforts of salespeople will not necessarily bear fruit quickly enough to generate the sales and profit equivalent to their salaries, commissions, and the like. This means you will need to be careful on two counts. First, you need to have sufficient dollars available to meet this salary requirement until the sales effort can generate sufficient dollars to handle this cost. Second, you must have some sense of how long it will take for the sales effort to convert this sales energy into real dollars. You will need to develop a time line that is fairly dependable to ensure that the business does not run out of money before this equation becomes positive.

Cutting expenses

Another way of increasing profit, apart from increasing sales or producing product in a more expeditious or cost-saving way, is to cut the expenses of doing business—your administrative expenses.

In a home-based business, the single most expensive cost of doing business is usually absent—the rent for the business premises. Some businesses, of course, are more likely prospects for this than others. Sometimes the location or the size of the premises can be changed, and this will result in a lower cost. Not all businesses are good prospects for this either.

Outsourcing

Whether you are starting a business or maintaining one, you will recognize that certain aspects of the business are best done "in-house" by internal personnel, and other things are best, and most economically, done by "outsourcing"—having the job performed by outside personnel or companies. Handling payroll, with all the taxes that need to be accounted for, can be handled by outside companies. If the payroll is extremely small, it might be more economical to handle it yourself. Or, if the business is large enough to have a financial department or financial personnel, it might be more economical to handle it in-house. Bookkeeping and tax preparation would fall into a similar category.

Outsourcing the manufacture of parts, instead of trying to develop the capacity to do it all in-house, might be a better program with a greater degree of profit. Some manufacturers actually use outside distributors, which are essentially outside sales organizations. Much, of course, will depend on the particular industry, the size and scope of your business, and the method by which the greatest profit can be achieved.

There are new service companies available that will handle virtually every aspect of your business if you choose to go that route, leaving only those things based on the ingenuity or creativity of the owner. Many of these operations are referred to as "virtual offices."

It is a good idea to examine these many alternatives carefully, whether you are starting a business or merely maintaining its continuity. It is also true that these alternatives may come in handy as your business reaches different plateaus or different aspects of growth.

Diversity

Another aspect of business growth is the concept of reaching out for collateral products or services that may be appropriate to your basic customer needs. In the printing industry, for example, it became necessary—and appropriate due to the development of user-friendly equipment—for printers to enhance their product line to include prepress capability—typesetting and graphics—which had previously been considered a separate industry. The further sophistication of computer technology is now leading to printers being "on line," with the customer allowing words and concepts to be transmitted directly, without any paper actually changing hands.

Horizontal and vertical growth

Diversity can also mean opening outlets similar to your primary location to reach more and more customers. This is called horizontal expansion. This type of business growth—the creation of additional outlets—can be effected in a variety of ways, one of which is franchising. It is important, however, to recognize that this should never be considered a collateral function to an existing, successful business. Franchising requires a separate reservoir of money, personnel, creativity, and energy. It is a separate business in itself and must be given the appropriate tools with which to make it grow. It requires special attention to detail and to the franchise relationship, on which its growth is clearly predicated. For more detail on this, see Chapter 7, *Franchise or Otherwise*.

Diversity can also mean manufacturing more parts that were formerly outsourced. This is called vertical expansion. This can lead to a greater profit by putting more capability under the same roof. A caution about vertical expansion should also be recognized. Trying to be the "one-stop station" under whose roof all aspects of the business can be maintained can be dangerous. Oftentimes it might be less expensive to use an outside sales organization than to try to build one internally. Those who handle only sales are most likely to understand how it should be operated on a more cost-effective basis. Learning a new aspect of business under your own roof might have an extensive—and costly—learning curve.

Each of these moves, of course, takes you back to the chicken/egg problem, the answer to which is critical to any aspect of growth that can be appropriately converted to profit.

There is no magic out there—no way to guarantee a fast track to success. But it is the caution you exercise that will allow you to maintain your competitive edge in the marketplace.

Key points

- Don't make the mistake of underselling your product or service as a "good beginning" to increased sales.

- Make sure your confidence has a strong relationship to the reality of your industry.

- Be sure you have sufficient working capital when hiring a salesperson to initiate a sales program.

- Outsourcing can be a dramatic way of saving dollars.

- Be careful that vertical or horizontal expansion is consistent with your available capital resources.

Worksheet

- Businesses are normally broken down into a pie chart of four basic parts. What are they?

- Why is leasing equipment often a better program than purchasing?

- What are the dangers of signing a leasing contract?

- What is the basic advantage of a home based business?

- What is the difference between vertical and horizontal expansion?

17

Real People:
The Entrepreneur,
The Investor, The Lender

All philosophical axioms aside, most people are more interested in—and will give more weight to—real life examples. This chapter is devoted to three such interviews. The first is with an entrepreneur who has experienced the peaks and valleys of business ownership—success and failure. The second is with an investor whose experiences over a lifetime have afforded him the knowledge to know when to invest, when to expect success, and when to predict failure. The third is with a banker who is on the front line of lending to the small business person and who can explain in simple terms the whys and wherefores of the lending paradox.

Interview with Scott Adler, CEO of Shoe Wiz Corporation

It is always disturbing when a self-styled genius who made millions of dollars stands up in front of an audience and tells people just how he did it—saying, essentially, that everything he ever touched turned to gold. It is of particular interest that these same people never made a bad business decision, never made an unwise investment, never fell in with the proverbial den of thieves, and never just got unlucky. Can you imagine that?!

Most successful people have a sad tale of woe tucked somewhere in their bag of experience. Many have said that, were it not for those unfortunate moments, they wouldn't have had the ability to handle the day-to-day problems that surface during the course of any subsequent successful venture. These are the people you want to meet. These are the people to whom you should pay attention. These are the people who can give you the tools to construct your own adventures with strong foundations to weather the adversities that are inherent in every business.

The hallmarks of success and the signposts of danger

Scott Adler started a business back in 1982. His business venture generated some very dynamic publicity. As a result, he was solicited by just about everyone. He was advised to surround himself with all the heavyweights. He got involved on the fast-moving train of success, moving more quickly all the time. He followed advice from the professionals. The company managed to generate half a million dollars from some local investors. Money was coming in and money was going out. Investors were happy to jump on the train. The names of some of these investors could be found on page one of the newspapers almost any day of the week.

Then one of the professionals tried to take over the company. Scott managed to fight off this takeover. Then another one of the professionals was successful in taking the company public. They sold 40% of the company for two and a half million dollars, even though the company had barely started its basic operation. More money poured in. Judgments were made about bringing in some more heavyweights to bolster the management group.

New management brought in new ideas, created new directions, and established new momentum.

Then the train stopped.

One of the giant companies on which Scott's operation was dependent for its raw materials became a competitor to some of his locations. Scott's company generated the greater success in those competitive marketplaces. The other company lost out. Then the other company refused to continue doing business with Scott's company. As Scott says, *"We won the battles, but we lost the war."*

Finally, Scott resigned from his own company. Two and a half years later, the company went bankrupt. The heavyweights had won. They had lifted him up, carried him along, and dropped him on his head. Scott has become philosophical about the train ride. His comment: *"It was the greatest learning experience of my life."*

There are a lot of lessons to learn from this story. Some are obvious; some are more subtle. The man who tells the story is a man of strength who didn't give up after his dream turned to smoke. He used the lessons as the foundation for a new business venture. He is more careful about the people who surround him. He is optimistic about the future, but only within the realm of reality. He is now succeeding—again. These are the real lessons to learn!

People still represent the most important element in a business

Having shared a very personal story, Scott is happy to discuss his present business from the standpoint of those things that can help a buyer understand the elements necessary to ensure success. One of these basics is hiring good people.

Scott now owns a chain of retail outlets, operated by managers hired by him. Since each business requires a cash investment of about $175,000, Scott has insisted on maintaining strong management criteria as well as creating a basic supervisory approach to continuing operations.

The name of the business is Shoe Wiz. The concept involves the repair of shoes, boots, and leather goods, and the sale of collateral items to service the concept. It is basically a cash business. The positive side of this is that, as an owner, you don't have to worry about collecting receivables. The negative side is that, without being on premises all the time—obviously impossible when you have a chain of outlets—you are not in control of the cash flow of the business. Dollars have a way of slipping through the cracks—sometimes through embezzlement, sometimes through inadvertence, bad pricing policy, unreasonable discounting, etc. Scott is certainly aware of the problem. As he says:

> *"It's hard to believe that, in a simple business like this one, there are over 800 different items in inventory. We had to develop a computer system just to keep track of the inventory. A side advantage, of course, is that we developed better controls throughout the entire business as a result. It is a stable business, very predictable."*

In terms of hiring personnel, Scott's answer involved a variety of issues:

> *"Even though we don't require outside selling, it is important that our people enjoy dealing with the public, be reasonably well organized, and take some initiative. I have no quarrel with anybody's religious or preferential dress, but I want uniformity when they are working in the shop."*

On the subject of drug or alcohol abuse, Scott has taken a somewhat different attitude:

> *"I normally don't ask an applicant that question on the interview. I just make it clear that their job depends on their attitude and performance. Of course, I check their former employers and other references, but the real key is their attitude and performance. We give them a one-year probationary period. This is in writing so there is no mistake about it. If they had a problem before but they don't have it anymore, they could become long-term employees."*

The paradox of prior experience

What about prior experience? Scott's answer reflects the attitude of most entrepreneurs:

"It's very interesting. If their prior experience is in retailing generally, it can serve both the employee and the business very well. If their prior experience is in the shoe repair business, this can be good or bad. It can shortcut a lot of their training. Or it could mean that they've developed a lot of bad habits. Some of these habits are difficult, if not impossible, to break.

"You just have to watch, wait, and then decide what kind of manager you've got. Part of it has to do with luck and part of it has to do with good training and good supervision, without interfering with either their daily activity or their own initiative."

Salesperson or craftsperson

The next question is typically asked of people who operate more than one retail location. The question is whether the managers can operate the equipment and whether they were encouraged to do this:

"A good repair craftsman can do a superb job without wasting any time. A good manager can smile warmly, price accurately, maintain a clean operation, and keep a good hold on getting things done in timely fashion. But, he or she is normally not a good repair craftsman.

The finest managers don't operate the equipment. Since we have enough stores within a given geography, it is up to the manager to find a replacement, temporary or permanent, when it becomes necessary. We find that this division of talent and responsibility is the best approach. It is possible, and sometimes appropriate, to have the technician take care of the customer. However, as a general rule, we do not encourage it. Having the repair craftsman take over the counter is not encouraged either, for the same reasons.

It's interesting that many businesspeople find they can most easily increase their business by dealing with existing customers. With the manager at the counter, the likelihood of upgrading the sale is much greater than having the technician merely close the cash drawer after getting paid." As Scott says, *"This suggestive selling is responsible for a good portion of every month's revenues."*

Formal education is not necessarily the key

It is always interesting that, when talking about business, questions of education and background are normally considered essential. Notwithstanding our standards that college education is necessary for certain job categories and that high school education is mandatory for just about everything else, the business world requires good sense. Certainly, a businessperson should be able to add and subtract, spell reasonably well, and have certain verbal skills. But good sense is the key to good business. After all, good sense tells us when something's wrong; good sense tells us when we should seek advice from a more experienced source.

As Scott says,

> *"We compensate our managers on the basis of store performance. They all know that more sales and lower costs mean more profit. And that profit means money in their pockets. They all know that more time taken to finish a job means a higher labor cost and higher labor costs mean less profit. And that less profit means less money in their bonus envelopes. They all know that wasting product means more money for inventory and that higher cost of product means less profit. And that less profit means less money in their bonus envelopes. It is amazing how fast the uneducated become sophisticated when the dollar is based on their understanding of the basics."*

The best incentive

> *"It is also interesting to note that a good manager knows how fast he or she is using product and when it would be appropriate to reorder based on time of delivery, etc. Certainly, we take the responsibility for the ordering, but we do it based on the manager's response to available inventory measured against usage. The managers develop an intuitive sense quickly and make good decisions when profit is the goal."*

Scott doesn't seem to feel that gender, age, or family situations have much to do with the effectiveness of a manager. His only comment was in the nature of a statistic.

> *"Most of our managers are married and take their jobs quite seriously. They make a base salary of about $36,000 per year, and with bonuses they can average between $40,000 and $45,000 per year." (dollar values from 1998)*

The genesis of the modern-day workforce

Another important question is whether a husband and wife team are generally a good idea. Scott's answer was a bit of a surprise:

"Some husband and wife teams working together have a tendency to think in terms of how they can treat the profit as their own. Although this has its positive side, it can also be a negative. Some of them wonder after a short while why the absent owner, notwithstanding his financial involvement, should be entitled to any part of the profit generated by the proverbial sweat of their brows. This becomes a clear and present danger. Even the closest supervision and the most sophisticated computer technology is not going to protect against this attitude. That's why I said early on "their jobs depend on their attitudes and their performance." I feel very strongly about the word attitude. It's really what success is all about!"

Take the gamble out of the game—in every possible way

Scott was asked if he had considered the idea of franchising the business, especially since he had already proven the concept by opening and maintaining some seventeen shops. His answer should represent a strong caution to anyone who ever owned a business and dreamed of building a dynasty:

"I've already had a taste of that game. Most people don't realize that creating a franchise means taking on a giant responsibility to the people who invest their money. Right now, I only owe that responsibility to myself and my shareholders. If and when I'm satisfied that most of the gamble is out of the game, I certainly might consider the building of a franchise network."

It's too bad all businesspeople don't have the standard of ethics Scott has. "Take the gamble out of the game," indeed!

A view to investment—from an investor's perspective: Who is Bill LeVine?

The PIP story tells us what we need to know about the man, and his success. Bill LeVine was a printer who started selling printed material while he was still in high school. He proceeded to build a successful commercial printing plant. He was always looking for innovation in his industry. One day he found a new item at a trade show—a piece of equipment that could make a paper printing plate for pennies (instead of many dollars) and could do it in minutes, without any expertise (instead of the technically oriented and time-consuming method of "etching" a metal plate). He bought one. Then he put it together with a printing machine in the window of his commercial shop to show the passersby how a printing job could be done, from beginning to end, in minutes. The public loved it. Bill recognized the utility of it. He opened a shop that utilized this new combination of equipment. The shop did *Printing While You Wait.* Then he opened another. Then another. The concept was more than just interesting and exciting. It worked. His original commercial printing plant was called Postal Press. The new concept was called Postal *Instant* Press (currently known in the business community as PIP Printing). It made sense. But, more than that, it made money!

An investor/advisor

"It was interesting to me in the early days that successful businessmen would come to me for business advice. I guess the fact that I was older had a lot to do with it. After all, I didn't even start my own business until I was in my late forties. The rest of the managers and owners, who were always at the same meetings, were at least ten years younger. I know the white hair had a lot to do with it.

"These days, I feel a lot more comfortable about giving some answers. Sure, I've made plenty of mistakes. As an investor, I'm batting about .333. Not bad for a baseball player, but my banker wishes I did better. On the other hand, I know a little about business now and I know that .333 isn't bad. When one of them works, it usually works well and makes up for the ones that didn't.

"It's really too bad most people can't afford to lose. That makes it tough. That's why I always recommend you invest only about 20% of what you've got available. If you win, it's a bonus; if you lose, it's not a tragedy."

Bill LeVine is a somewhat unique individual in the sense that he created a successful independent business, and then he created a successful franchise business. He is now in a position to be able to recognize the best of both worlds. Bill currently serves on the boards of diverse companies, independent as well as franchised, public as well as private. He also has the unique perspective of serving on the board of the Mellon First Business Bank in Los Angeles, which has capital in excess of one billion dollars. His experience gives import to his advice.

You always need more than you think you do

Bill feels that many entrepreneurs are more interested in security these days than they were twenty years ago. People used to have security in their jobs. When they decided to go into business, it was for the purpose of building a retirement and not having to answer to the boss. Today, people no longer feel secure in their jobs; they are going into business to find security more than anything else.

A friend of Bill's came to him and talked about having $30,000 to invest in a new business venture. Bill's answer: *"Oh, hell. That's not all you need. You need five times that amount!"* Although Bill's basic philosophy is that you should invest only a portion of the cash you have available, he's not suggesting that you save the money for a rainy day. His concept of investment is that you should keep the balance for a working capital reservoir and a protection fund.

In Bill's words, *"Business today has become very sophisticated. You cannot embark on that adventure if you are short of experience, short of ability, or short of cash. But, cash can buy experience and ability if necessary. It's a good idea to have enough to draw from when an emergency arises."*

Another friend of Bill's from Denver said he had $48,000 because he figured he'd need a year to get to break-even in his new business. Bill's conservative observation was, *"What if you don't make it work within a year? You need a minimum of $100,000 so you can last two years if you have to."* This kind of advice, coming from someone's father, often falls on deaf ears. When this advice comes from Bill LeVine, the listener ought to keep both ears open!

Bill's philosophy is consistent all the way to the bank. Although the loan officer tends to all the necessary paperwork, it is the board that makes decisions about loans to businesspeople. If a businessperson asks for $500,000, Bill looks carefully to see if the applicant has the equity to borrow $750,000, just in case the business plan misses some unexpected contingencies. Bill also looks carefully at the cash flow of the business to ensure that *"the payments don't strangle him before he has a chance to get off the ground."* Bill not only wants the bank's dollars to be safe; he wants the business to succeed.

Getting ready for growth: A big key

It is interesting that Bill reflects on his mistakes with a sense of learning. He remembers growing so fast in his franchise business, back in 1969, that he had to put a stop on sales for a time to retrench. It isn't the usual story but it serves as a lesson that even success has its dynamic aspects, negative as well as positive. One of the lessons to which Bill can now attest: *"It is maintaining the equilibrium of growth and support for that growth that serves the stability of the business to best advantage."*

Part of this lesson is in another of Bill's stories—the story of a successful business that went into bankruptcy. The owner of a successful business was sold a bill of goods, as the old saying goes, by a franchise consultant. They set up a franchise; they got investors; they sold franchises; they didn't maintain *"the equilibrium of growth and support for that growth"*; they went bankrupt! The positive side of that story is that, after the debacle, the original owner found another good business idea and proceeded to build it into another successful business. If anything should substantiate the philosophy that, as Yogi Berra phrased it, "it ain't over 'til it's over," this should.

Even more than that, Bill comments, *"If you have the ability and the stamina, you can survive and prosper in the face of adversity, bad advice, and an occasional disaster."* It's a good story to remember.

Know what your real goals are

One of the suggestions Bill makes about today's entrepreneur is that he needs to know more about his goals than about a particular business. One person can buy a shoe repair shop that has sales of $25,000 a month with a 25% profit. The owner will have to get his hands dirty fixing and shining, but he won't have to worry about going out to meet the public to sell the product. If the goal is a secure living, and you don't mind getting your hands dirty, you have found an ideal situation.

Other people come to the table looking for an opportunity to build a dynasty. This requires an entirely different mindset, a different set of abilities, and an inclination to a much more unstable future, rather than the security of fixing and shining and depositing money in the bank every week. As Bill says, *"Neither candidate is wrong. Each is right for the purpose of attaining his or her own personal goal."*

Bill makes a severe distinction between the operational investor and the passive investor. *"If you are going to get involved as a passive investor, and you intend to live on the income, the minimum required for an investment in today's economy is probably $500,000. If you are investing anything less than that, you ought to be considering an active participation in the business."*

What does the future hold?

When asked about the next ten years, Bill is positive but concerned. He knows that, in the American psyche, there is enough innovation and creativity to start the computer revolution again. He is frank enough to say that he just doesn't know what the replacement for the computer will be. He recognizes that competition has created a much different marketplace than existed in the '60s, '70s, '80s, and '90s. *"It's going to be about people getting out and talking to people. Unless you have an exclusive product, service, or market area, you must be a lot more marketing oriented than was necessary 20 years ago."* Bill suggests even further, *"If you are not marketing oriented, it would be a good idea to have a partner who is, or to have enough money in the pot to hire someone who is. In today's market, you've just got to know when to use a loss leader like a drugstore might, or purchase extra shelf space like Coca-Cola, or advertise aggressively like McDonald's—who, by the way, controls a substantial portion of the nation's fast food business due to that advertising strength."*

But a lot of readers are interested in how Bill got to where he is. Is there a secret? Is there a lot left to chance? Is it all done with a carefully orchestrated plan? Or is it sometimes, as Bill himself says, *"being in the right place at the right time. And being prepared for it when you get there."* The fact is, he needed to take a chance; he gambled. He was willing to make the sacrifices to do what was necessary to succeed.

Capitalizing on the concept

The idea of franchising the concept came to Bill from many sources. Finally, he looked into the possibility and, in one day at a franchise show, sold five franchises. Sure, he was in the right place at the right time. But nobody else made it happen. *He* did!

Then he proved that it takes a little bit more than just being in the right place at the right time. He paid attention to what kind of people bought his franchises. He taught them with attention to detail and followed that up with careful supervision. He paid attention to the franchisees. He hired people to work with him and insisted that they work with the same ethic that he did. He helped some franchisees with advice; he helped others with money. It all paid off. The company went public and became the largest printing franchise in the world. Sure, he was in the right place at the right time. But nobody else made it happen. *He* did!

Bill was 46 years old when he started the franchise business.

Interview with Bill Unrein, Vice President of Bank One, Boulder, Colorado

It is always surprising how many interviews are scheduled with presidents of companies about the intricacies of a corporate advertising campaign. Wouldn't it be more appropriate to discuss the matter with the advertising manager, whose life is totally immersed in the concepts of maximizing the corporate advertising dollar? Isn't this the person who can give you the real story?

Indeed, what about the interview with the president of a bank who, to his credit, has a myriad of responsibilities far removed from the emotional trauma of the customer who wants to borrow money to maintain the health and welfare of his family? Why not ask the person whose job it is to analyze the application and make the all-important preliminary judgment as to whether this particular loan application ought to go any farther up the approval ladder? This is the interview that follows!

Bill Unrein has been in the commercial lending business for eighteen years. He has an optimistic view toward the rise and success of small business, but in terms of lending philosophy he is still a banker of the conservative school.

The somewhat singular role of the bank

As Bill says, *"Taking a chance on the success of a business by taking an equity position in the company is the role of a venture capital partner. The traditional commercial bank can't do this. It is not allowed by law to be an equity partner. Some banks have spin-offs that are venture capital entities, and business can be referred from one firm to the other."* Bill is quick to caution, however, *"There cannot be any direct ties between the two entities."*

The bank:
A lender or a financial consultant

The question comes up, then, as to whether the bank serves as a lender or merely as a financial consultant that will extend credit only when there is an appropriate portfolio of hard assets to support the dollars involved. Bill's answer is consistent. *"Our role as a financial institution is a unique one from organization to organization, but certain factors don't change. It is the same general approach with a little different twist. If we are dealing with an existing company, for example, with good earnings, solid assets, and a strong earning history, we will extend credit to them to acquire assets, get over a bad patch, or expand their market potential. We will, of course, still require sufficient assets to support the loan. In some cases, for example, we may take an assignment of receivables to secure our position for a short-term loan. At the very least, the personal signatures of the principals is evidence that the owners of the business consider the loan to be secure. This is what commercial banks are all about."*

The two basic prerequisites

Bill continues, suggesting an analogy. *"Just as with the financing of a home purchase, the bank must assess two important elements: 1) whether there is sufficient equity in the property to warrant the gross amount of the loan, 2) whether the cash flow of the borrower is strong enough to meet the monthly payment obligation. To use the jargon of the industry, the bank needs to assess the credit risk. This would be the case in practically every instance."*

Government backup support

On the subject of smaller businesses, particularly acquisition of a small business, Bill draws the analogy a little tighter. *"Lending in the area of small business goes back to my statement that 'it is the same general approach with a little different twist.' Let me say, to begin with, that the SBA (the Small Business Administration) has been a big factor in the growth of this area. After all, they will guarantee up to 90% on new loans and up to 80% in a refinancing situation. Actually, the biggest consideration probably comes from the CRA (the Community Reinvestment Act), which requires that banks make funds available to low to moderate income groups. Lending in this area has become a very big business. In one particular year, we actually ran out of loanable funds. This, of course, also causes us to be more selective in the loans we make."*

In terms of specifics, Bill acknowledges the bank's basic philosophy. *"When we extend a three-, five-, or seven-year loan to an established customer, the bank wants hard assets in the background. If we are dealing with the purchaser of a business who is not an established customer, the assets must be a lot closer to our control."* In other words, from a practical standpoint, Bill makes it clear that the bank wants to be in a secure position should any of the potential disasters of a small business become a reality.

The extent of the bank's expertise

In all fairness, the bank's expertise does not lie in the area of the business itself. Small businesses are subject to a variety of potential dangers, including, among others, the fickle nature of the customer, the illness of the owner or of a key employee, the opening of a strong competitor, and new concept or product in the particular industry. These are the things over which the bank has no control and, in many cases, of which they have no knowledge until it's too late. This is why Bill tried to stress that the bank must be a lender, not an investor.

The alternatives to hard assets as security

There are, of course, many other ways to secure the loan besides just the hard assets. As Bill suggests, *"I see a number of alternative situations in the small business area. It is not unusual for a buyer to speak of his uncle in Illinois who would be happy to support the business purchase. The bank could get an irrevocable letter of credit from the uncle's bank, or a personal signature of the uncle or, perhaps, real property of the uncle on which the bank could take a trust deed. Any one of those alternatives might support the loan."* It is certainly clear from these alternatives that the bank is not taking any chances. Bill puts it into bank phraseology by saying, *"When you're dealing with a small business acquisition, you've got to have either outside support, a cosigner, hard assets, or a guarantee by the SBA. In other words, there must be some kind of credit enhancement."*

Examining a small service business, for example, that has a good cash flow, a good credit history, good projections, a solid industry, and a good competitive position but no substantial collateral as security for a loan, Bill gives us essentially the same answer. *"You must remember that the bank is not here to take an equity position. The bank cannot be considered an investor, a gambler. That's a much different role, which, as I've mentioned, can only be adopted by a much different kind of institution."*

The question becomes, then, Is the bank really a lender or merely a financial advisor that will make cash available only when something (like assets) *separate but equal* represent the quid pro quo? Bill explains. *"Sometimes an existing business customer wants to acquire a competitor, and we will examine with him just what the benefits are: Does it make business sense in the short term and the long term? What are the ultimate advantages? What are the risks on the downside? This does certainly put us into the role of a financial advisor. Although we also offer analysis and advice to our customers who might be selling a business, we're usually dealing with a buyer who wants to put our money up to buy the business. In this context, we are back in the lender position.*

On the positive side, one trend we've noticed is that most borrowers have become more conservative in their own right. They really would like to minimize their borrowing. I wouldn't be surprised if a lot of this thinking comes from the big companies downsizing in the face of the recession at the end of the eighties. As small business people watch the big companies trying to operate with a leaner staff and spend less money, they also are trying to picture their own ventures with smaller capitalization, smaller staff, and bigger profits. It's probably a good sign."

A real-life story

The best way to pull all the lending philosophies together is to present an example. Bill gives us the benefit of one that actually happened. *"A Texas businessman wanted to move* *to Boulder and acquire a small business comprised of three to four stores. Our bank was referred to the buyer by his own bank in Texas, so we were reasonably comfortable with the financial history of the borrower. The seller was looking for a little too much money and the buyer wanted to structure a loan of about $600,000 over a five- to seven-year period. The cash flow of the business appeared to be strong enough to handle the payment schedule, but the assets had a value of only about one-half the amount of the anticipated loan. In this case, we did in fact act a little in the capacity of a financial consultant—or, saying it another way, as a financial negotiator. We asked the seller if he would carry some of the debt. We actually suggested he take one-half of the obligation. The seller was not interested in doing this. He wanted to cash out. We then tried to negotiate the price between the buyer and the seller in an attempt to work out a purchase arrangement that would work for both parties. We also spoke with the SBA in the hope of getting 80–90% of the loan guaranteed. This, of course, would have allowed us to fund the purchase. Unfortunately, we were unsuccessful in these attempts, and the deal did not go through."*

One of the keys appears to be that the banking institution is not going to be a part of the business to be purchased. The bank would certainly like to make a good loan, but they are not in the position of making a business investment. As Bill says, *"The bank's business is lending money and getting it back. It doesn't understand every business it lends money to—and doesn't pretend to. Other businesses are not our business. Banking is our only business—and we try to do it well for the benefit of our depositors and our investors."*

That really appears to be the bottom line!

Key points

- Hiring good people and maintaining supervision of those people are two keys to success.

- Maintaining the equilibrium of growth and support for that growth is mandatory for continuity of a business.

- Make sure you have enough of a cash reservoir for both operating capital and emergencies.

- Always anticipate that growth may take twice the time you expect.

- Remember that the bank's role is not being your partner—only your lender.

Worksheet

- Why is an employee's "attitude" more important than his or her education?

- What is a potential problem with husband and wife teams?

- What is an appropriate expectation for an investor in terms of percentage of successes versus failures?

- Why is it always appropriate to borrow more than you actually need?

- Why is a bank consistently looking for hard assets when lending to a small business?

$\boxed{18}$

How to Value a Business

[*Author's Note: Since most of the preparation for a sale is the responsibility of the seller, this chapter is written primarily from the seller's perspective. Reading this is the best preparation for a buyer in terms of understanding both sides of the negotiating table.*]

The necessary assumptions

To value a business properly, you must make two basic assumptions, both of which are normally true. The first is that the buyer, after the purchase, has probably exhausted all or most of his or her available financial resources. This is usually true because most buyers of small businesses follow the philosophy that the greater the investment, the greater the return. As a result, they will normally invest as much as they can. Whether this philosophy has any basis in fact is subject to further examination. But the fact is that most buyers invest this way.

The second assumption is that the buyer has made a substantial down payment rather than pay all cash for the business. This means that the balance of the purchase price will be paid to the seller in incremental payments over an extended period of time. It is very unusual in today's business marketplace for a business to be sold for "all cash." There are disadvantages to both buyer and seller, as will be further examined in this chapter.

What the buyer needs to handle

If you accept the above two assumptions, you are left in a situation where the buyer must depend on the cash flow of the acquired business to handle the two problems the buyer needs to address: 1) taking care of his or her family needs, and 2) making the periodic (normally monthly) payments to the seller.

Although there are a variety of elements that must also be taken into consideration—not the least of which involves the tax implications of the purchase—you now have the basic assumptions of business valuation in hand.

Discretionary cash flow

Discretionary cash flow is the money left over after paying all the expenses necessary to properly operate the business. You must first decide how much money you, the buyer, need to take care of your family. When you deduct this from the discretionary cash flow of the business, the balance remaining is the amount that can be used to pay the balance of the purchase price to the seller.

The following example may be helpful.

1. The discretionary cash flow of the business is $80,000 per year.
2. The salary necessary for the buyer to handle the needs of the family is $30,000 per year.
3. The balance of the $50,000 will be used to pay the seller the balance of the purchase price.

If the $50,000 is paid to the seller each year for 10 years, the value of the business is probably about $300,000. The reason for this is that to fully amortize—i.e., pay the principal sum and the interest at 10% over a period of ten years—a purchase price of $300,000 would require an annual payment of $47,900 per year.

Since the amount available from the discretionary cash flow is $50,000 per year, it would appear there is enough money to make the annual payments based on a purchase price of $300,000 and still have sufficient money available to satisfy the salary requirements of the buyer. In other words, it works! For more information on this concept, read the book *The Secrets to Buying and Selling a Business,* referenced at the close of this chapter.

Finding the discretionary cash flow

You should be looking at your P&L (profit and loss statement, also called an income statement) to find your discretionary cash flow (DCF). You may also need to refer to your balance sheet to clarify some questions on your P&L. See Chapter 12, *Understanding Your Income Statement* for a further explanation of this.

Converting your IRS presentation for selling purposes

You will normally be preparing your P&L for purposes of substantiating your tax position to the Internal Revenue Service. You or your accountant will prepare the P&L in such a way as to take full advantage of the deductions allowed by the government. In this way, you will be creating as small a profit (DCF) as possible to minimize the income taxes you will ultimately be obliged to pay.

On the other hand, presenting this same financial picture to a potential buyer will allow only a minimal selling price and will be totally unfair to the seller. Many of these deductions will not be part of the buyer's cash requirements for operating the business after the sale. If they are not, then they should "fall" to the bottom line—net profit of the business—for valuation purposes.

Costs necessary to properly operate the business

The reason for this strange dichotomy is that there are three basic cost factors allowed by the government as legitimate business deductions that will not be inherited by the buyer as necessary costs of operating the business. These include the following:

1. Depreciation and amortization: Although these are allowable as expenses against sales, thereby lowering the profit on which taxes are assessed, they are noncash items. That is, the business will not have to pay this amount in cash during the course of the year. See Chapter 1, *The Financial Picture* for a discussion of depreciation.
2. Nonrecurring expenses: The seller is entitled to deduct expenses of the sale, including the lawyer's, accountant's, and broker's fees. In addition, the seller may have purchased a computer, for example, so the buyer will not have to buy one after the sale. These are deductions for tax purposes that the buyer will not have to pay for after the sale, as operating expenses of the business.
3. Personal expenses: The seller may have taken a "helpful" trip to Europe ("educational" trip under IRS guidelines) during which he or she visited competitive operations. The visitations might qualify the expenses of the trip as a deductible business expense even though the seller's primary purpose might have been to take a holiday. The buyer will not be obliged to duplicate this trip as a *necessary* business operating expense.

These items should be deducted from the expense side of the P&L and "dropped" to the bottom line, becoming a part of the DCF. In turn, this will represent a much more realistic picture of what the actual discretionary cash flow (DCF) of the business can really afford to pay in terms of salary to the buyer and payments to the seller.

Selling for cash

Although it is certainly possible to sell or buy a business for "all cash," there are good reasons for both buyer and seller to carefully consider the negative aspects involved in such a purchase.

From the seller's perspective, there are three practical problems to consider.

1. The capital gains tax will be payable in full during the year of the sale because the seller received all of the money in that year.
2. The buyer, if paying all cash, will certainly expect, and be entitled, to pay much less than the asking price of the business. Although this is not always true—and depends on the relative negotiating positions of buyer and seller—there is a certain rationale for this perspective.
3. The current interest percentage this cash payment will ultimately generate as a passive investment in the open market is quite likely to be considerably less than the seller might expect if the seller "carried" the balance of the purchase price over a period of time after taking only a down payment. After all, "carrying" the balance of the purchase price involves some degree of risk. This risk usually converts to a higher interest rate than that generated by a more secure passive investment.

Seller's advantage

The positive side, of course, is that the seller will not be accepting the risk of collecting the balance if it is an all cash sale. The seller may actually consider the sale consummated and go on to other fields of endeavor without any notion of "looking over his or her shoulder."

Buyer's disadvantage

From the buyer's perspective, there is an important reason to avoid such a purchase. The buyer who pays all cash loses any leverage he or she might otherwise have had to protect against any misrepresentations, intentional or otherwise, of which the seller may be guilty. In addition, the seller, having been completely paid, loses all incentive to have a long transition period or to help the buyer during those early takeover stages when experience can save many dollars and help ensure the continuity of the business. The seller who collects the balance of the purchase price over an extended period of time is likely to be a lot more careful about transitioning the business to the buyer in every way that can help ensure a successful takeover.

So long as the buyer follows the philosophy that *the business should pay for itself*—that is, the cash flow (DCF) should support the buyer's needs as well as the payment schedule to the seller—there is little advantage to paying cash, and there are many negatives that would logically dictate otherwise.

The down payment

Although the value of a business should theoretically have little to do with the down payment, as a practical matter it does. There is certainly a minimum down payment that a smart seller will demand, for two reasons:

1. It is often necessary for the seller to meet certain closing expenses in addition to dollars owed, for a variety of reasons. The seller will often depend on a certain minimum down payment to accommodate these expenses, as well as the all-important tax implications.
2. Also, most sellers feel that a minimum down payment should be required if the seller is going to give up the prerogatives of ownership and accept the risk of collecting the balance of the purchase price.

From the seller's perspective, a minimum down payment is likely to be in the vicinity of about 20%. If the buyer is willing to make a greater down payment, it is likely that the buyer will expect something in return—normally a lower purchase price, a lower interest rate, or the like.

The buyer's bonus with a bigger down payment

The most significant aspect of the down payment, however, is that if the value has been determined and the length of time for the balance to be paid has been agreed on, then

(a) the larger the down payment,
(b) the smaller the balance to be paid,
(c) the lower the annual payments, and
(d) the more "salary" available to the buyer out of the DCF.

Remember, during all of these calculations, the DCF remains the same. The following example might be helpful.

	Case 1	Case 2
Purchase Price:	$300,000	$300,000
	10-year note @ 10%	10-year note @ 10%
Down Payment:	20%: $60,000	40%: $120,000
Balance of Note:	$240,000	$180,000
DCF:	$50,000	$50,000
Annual Note Payments:	$38,000	$28,500
Annual Salary to Buyer after the Sale:	$42,000	$51,500
	($30,000 plus the	($30,000 plus the
	additional $12,000)	additional $21,500)
	($50,000 − $38,000)	($50,000 − $28,500)

Working capital

Any examination of business valuation must include a discussion of working capital. Most small businesses are sold based on the seller retaining both the obligation to pay the payables as well as the prerogative of collecting the receivables for work already done or product already sold. This is not always the case, but it is usually the case. Some businesses will require a working capital reservoir to handle the expenses for work done while waiting for the work to be paid for.

In the printing business, for example, IBM may place an order for a substantial amount of money. They will expect the order to be produced and delivered in two weeks. They may not actually make any payments for a period of six weeks. During this waiting period, the printer will have to buy paper and ink, and pay the presspeople, the rent, the lease payments on equipment, electricity, and the like, while all the time waiting for the bill (the receivable) to be paid. This is often referred to as the "receivable turnover period." It is perfectly normal for any business that is not an "all cash" business. An all cash business would be one where the bill is paid when the product or service is delivered—like a fast food operation.

A truly cash business will not necessarily need this reservoir, but it may require available cash reserves for other reasons—the purchase of new equipment, the replacement of inventory, and the like. Make sure you know if your acquisition will require this working capital base and, if so, how much will be appropriate!

The balloon note

Although payment arrangements for the purchase price of a business should not directly affect the valuation, in some cases it does. Following the assumption that the business must be able to pay for itself, and that the DCF must be able to pay the buyer's salary and fully amortize the balance of the seller's purchase price over a reasonable period of time, consider the following.

If the balance of the purchase price is $300,000 and it is agreed that $100,000 will be paid at the end of a period—say 10 years—then the monthly payments will only be amortizing $200,000, instead of $300,000. These payments will be lower than the payments necessary to amortize $300,000. This would allow the seller to increase the price of the business and still leave the buyer with enough money from the DCF to meet the monthly payments. This would allow a higher purchase price than what the valuation concept actually allows. Essentially, it means a payment schedule exceeding a ten-year program.

The question is, What happens when the $100,000 comes due at the end of the 10 years? The buyer will have to do one of three things: (a) pay the $100,000; (b) have the original seller—or another lender—loan the buyer the $100,000 (which means the payment schedule will be much longer than the original ten-year program), or (c) return the business to the seller after paying $200,000 and failing to pay the balance of the purchase price.

Robert Dunn ran across this problem when he decided to sell the business he had purchased before the end of the original payment schedule. He had owned it only eight years and had two years left on his Purchase Money Promissory Note (PMPN). The problem was that he needed to have a "new" payment schedule (a new, adjusted schedule) to include the balance owing on the promissory note as well as the balloon note of $100,000, which would come due in two years. He needed to negotiate this figure with the original owner in order to make a presentation to potential buyers who would be taking over the total (aggregate) obligation as part of the new purchase price. The buyers needed to know what their monthly payments would be after the down payment and how long before the obligation would be completely paid.

The original seller wouldn't negotiate a new schedule until a buyer was found. Robert found the buyers were not interested in discussing acquisition of a business when the payment schedule was "left up in the air." What this meant was that the buyer would have to negotiate with the original owner even after agreeing to a price with the seller. The balloon note situation created an unsolvable problem. The business was not sold.

Once a business has been valued, the DCF must be sufficient to meet a schedule of payments on the purchase price after a down payment. Using a balloon note to increase the purchase price allows the seller to get more than the value of the business. Buyer beware this type of presentation!

Key points

- A balloon payment will often be used to unfairly increase the selling price of a business.
- You must always reconstitute your "IRS P&L" for buyer presentation purposes.
- A substantial down payment should inure to the benefit of the buyer.
- The DCF must take care of the buyer's salary and the payment schedule on the PMPN representing the balance of a purchase price.
- Working capital is a good idea in most businesses. It is absolutely essential in a non-cash business to handle the "receivable turnover period."

Worksheet

- What is the "discretionary cash flow" of a business?
- Why is the P&L prepared for the IRS different from a "buyer presentation?"
- What are the three categories on the P&L that can be deleted in a buyer presentation?
- Why does the seller often prefer an "all cash" deal?
- Why does the buyer usually prefer to avoid an "all cash" deal?

[*Publisher's Note: For a much more definitive analysis of this question, both from the standpoint of the buyer as well as the seller, be sure to read* **The Secrets to Buying and Selling a Business,** *by Ira Nottonson, published by The Oasis Press, 1994, revised 1997.*]

19

The Art of Negotiating

The greatest misconception about "negotiating" is contained in the word "winning." Watching any sporting event will tell you that for every winner, you will invariably have one or more losers.

Do you care about the losers?

The question is, If you are a winner, do you care about the losers? In a sporting event, other than a moment of compassion or empathy, you probably won't. What about winning in business? Yes, there are times when winning becomes the primary goal. However, more often than not, in business, winning at the expense of someone else can have a dangerous backlash.

Take, for example, the sale of a business. The sellers want to get as much as they can and the buyers want to pay as little as possible. In the business marketplace today, most so-called "small businesses" are sold to buyers on the basis of a down payment, with the balance of the purchase price being paid over a period of time. This "balance" is represented by a promissory note. If the sale price is "too high," the business will either falter or collapse, because the buyers will not be able to maintain the business' continuity. In such an event the buyers will not be able to pay the balance of the purchase price because most buyers will have exhausted their own reservoir of dollars at the time of purchase. In such a case, did the sellers really win? The fact of the matter is that, with respect to the sale of businesses, there are parameters within which a purchase price can serve the interests of both parties without either feeling that an inequity has resulted from the negotiations (see Chapter 18, *How to Value a Business*).

Although it is true that sellers may sue buyers for the balance of the purchase price—or in some cases take the business back—experience will tell you that neither of these solutions will ever compare to collecting the balance of the purchase price in accordance with the terms of the original sale agreement.

Adjusting your expectations

If the negotiations lead to a situation where there is a winner at the expense of a loser, don't be surprised if the long-term result is that there are actually two losers. The goal of negotiating is not to win in the short term; it is to adjust your expectations to achieve a result satisfactory to both parties in the short term *and* the long term.

Trying to get the best of the other party in a negotiated relationship will often lead to the loser biding his or her time until the tables can be turned. The potential disaster makes the original winning very conjectural and, normally, a very short-lived success.

If you are at a basketball game or a track and field event, it is expected that there will be winners and losers. The confrontation is what brings the spectators back and causes them to support their team or their favorite athlete.

In the business world, today's negotiation is often a small part of a long-term relationship. It is in the positive aspects of those relationships that your business will find its ultimate success.

Backlash to the winner

In manufacturing businesses, where raw material is an essential element for survival, there are many source companies, each of which at any given time might carry its product at a particularly low price. Some manufacturers will leverage their buying power by negotiating for the lowest price and jumping from one source company to another to accomplish this. Up to a point, this is good business practice. Sometimes, however, the leverage—the pursuit of a better price—might be more based on principle rather than on substantial cost savings.

Occasionally, there will be (as there has been) a critical shortage of a particular raw material. Which customers will continue to receive their necessary allocation and which might not? The business marketplace is alive with "give and take." Being clever and exercising all your prerogatives might not always be the best approach for long-term success. Profit is certainly a key factor in the success of a business enterprise. It should not, however, be the sole element of your working guidelines for the long-term survival and success of your business.

Be careful, when negotiating, to understand the other party's position. If you fail to do this, the "success" of your negotiating may come back to haunt you. Today's negotiating success may be the beginning of tomorrow's negotiating failure. Much, of course, will depend on the need for an ongoing relationship with the other party. Sometimes it's a good idea to make concessions to the other side. It can generate positive results down the road. On the other hand, if you are negotiating the sale of your automobile, your negotiating need not consider a long-term relationship, providing you are being paid in cash at the time of the sale. In fact, you should not turn over possession of the automobile unless you are getting all cash at the time of the transfer. This sale represents a single moment in time. It is normally not the beginning of a long-term relationship.

Using the 10 point system

A good way to initiate your thinking and your negotiating posture is to pick the ten most important things you expect to accomplish. Establish a priority system in terms of importance to the short-term and long-term success of your business. Pick three items that you absolutely cannot afford to give up—those things that are critical to your business. Then pick the three least important items, which you can use for negotiating purposes—those items that are clearly not critical, but which could be helpful. Then establish a relative value for each of the four remaining in the middle. Your goal will be to get the items that are most important and to concede those items, if necessary, that are least important. The problem with many people is that they go into a negotiating situation thinking they must get all the points on their list. This is not negotiating. It is mandating. Make sure you understand the difference.

You don't have to cast this concept in concrete, but remember that adjusting your expectations is the key to negotiating.

Negotiating is not mandating

There is, of course, a point in all business relationships where you realize the goal will never become a reality. Mandating your goals or requirements will not do the trick. If you are unable to adjust your expectations to the point where you can concede what you can to get those items you need, then there is no deal and the negotiations are over. You must acknowledge when you have reached this point. It is appropriate at that stage to close the negotiating session with the understanding that all parties may choose to return at another time when the critical elements relative to each party may have changed. Mandating, even when you have the power to do so, may lead to a situation where the other side will merely wait for the tables to turn.

There are some situations that are merely not meant to be. The sales prices on a given business, even though perfectly legitimate and defensible, might not work for a particular buyer. There might not be enough down payment, enough cash for working capital, or enough dollars for additional inventory or equipment. Any number of reasons might leave the buyer without enough money left to maintain the business. On the other hand, by adjusting expectations, the seller may find many creative ways for the price to be paid and a deal to be struck.

Contracts with vendors or customers may just be too onerous for all parties to enjoy success. When this happens, STOP! Allow all parties to recognize the futility of further negotiations and wait for the business relationship to revive on another day. This kind of honesty today is a good predicate for a whole batch of tomorrows.

The glass top table

Negotiating is rarely successful when one party hides or misrepresents a fact that causes a deal to make. Recognition of this kind of negotiating can lead to litigation, or at least a loss of credibility in the marketplace. Keep everything on top of the table. It will take you a long way in your search for success as an entrepreneur. Once credibility is lost, even over a minor point, you may not be able to reestablish the trust, the kind of environment within which a successful negotiation can take place.

In the case of most long-term business relationships, it is appropriate to keep in mind that negotiating is normally the beginning of the game, not the end. Each party is expected to create a picture in a light most favorable to its side. This does not mean skewing the facts or misrepresenting any aspect of the business. If the buyer finds out about such a deception, the deal will certainly not be consummated. On the other hand, if the buyer doesn't find out until after the closing, the results can be even more devastating. One possible consequence is the buyer's failure to pay the balance of the purchase price, if there is such a balance. Another is litigation to have all payments returned. In some cases, where actual fraud is alleged, the alternatives become even more serious, with punitive damages being involved. (Punitive damages are normally assessed as punishment, as opposed to compensatory damages, which are designed to reimburse a party for actual money lost or spent.)

Case in point

Take the case of Barney, who owned a manufacturing business that was sold for $750,000. During the negotiations, in answer to a question raised by the buyer, Barney made a statement to the effect that "the return rate for defective product" was less than 1%.

After the sale, this statement was found to be quite misleading, since the return rate for defective product was historically closer to 10%. Barney's explanation was that although historically the 10% was accurate, this figure was irrelevant since all the problems causing defects had been solved, and recent production showed a defective percentage of less than 1%.

The buyer was not interested in gambling on the fact that production would continue with the lower defect percentage. The buyer had calculated the purchase price based on production costs with the lower defect percentage, and was entitled to rely on that as part of his calculations in determining the price of the business he was willing to pay. Whether he would have agreed to the same price if he had been given a different figure is unclear, but the answer to that question will never be known.

The buyer contended that he did not get the value he had paid for. Since a percentage of the purchase price was to be paid over an extended period of time, the buyer was able to exert a substantial negotiating position by threatening litigation and threatening not to pay the balance of the purchase price.

The interesting aspect of this "misrepresentation" is twofold: 1) It is unimportant whether the seller intended to deceive or whether his intentions were honorable, and 2) it is unimportant whether the misrepresentation would actually have adversely affected the buyer's business, his position in the marketplace, or his ultimate profit. The fact is that it gave the buyer a legitimate reason to renegotiate the original purchase price. However innocent your representation might appear to be during negotiations, keep in mind that buyers will always be looking for ammunition to shoot down a negotiated sale. Don't give your buyer any reason to renegotiate based on information that is unclear, ambiguous, or deceptive. However, keep in mind that minor representations, which could not conceivably affect the business in any way, are not subject to the same implications as those involved in this case. In the law, these "minor" representations are known as "de minimas." A court will not normally allow such a misrepresentation to affect an agreement. Usually, the defect must be substantial—*unless it was intentional.*

If you are represented by a consultant or an attorney during negotiations, it is likely that you will be advised to carefully examine the nature and quality of your representations. The professional does not want to be sued, either by the buyer for complicity in any deception—intentional or otherwise—or by you, the client, for allowing any misrepresentations to be made. Using your professional as part of your selling team is always a good idea.

Representing you, as the buyer, a professional will also be looking for any such misrepresentation that can injure you either in the short term or the long term.

Blinking eyes and red ties

There have been many books written and convention speakers continue to deliver exciting presentations about aspects of negotiating that are simply underwhelming. Some say you can always tell when someone is telling a lie because they blink faster than usual. The fact is that "the blink rate" is as diverse as the human animal itself. Some people may blink quickly when they're nervous, but others may blink quickly for no reason at all. Some experts will tell you to beware the individuals who move around in their chairs, who cross their legs, who uncross their legs, who tap on the table, who play with a pen or pencil, who scribble on paper, who smile too much, who don't smile at all, who pull their ears, scratch their noses and otherwise make noises or motions that give away their deepest emotional discomforts. Balderdash! If you ever sat at a poker table, you would see many of these same motions and they would likely be just as undeserving of careful scrutiny. Although body language is certainly a method of communicating, be careful not to overinterpret and make assessments that lead you to errors of judgment.

There are those who would advise you to position yourself carefully at a table. It is probably true that you should not sit at a table with the sun in your eyes, but be careful not to take these suggestions too much to heart. There is a somewhat flamboyant lawyer who had a very interesting office some years ago. His desk was positioned three steps up from the guest chairs in his office. There was a stained glass window behind his chair, and when the sun went down in late afternoons (the time he kept for most appointments) his head was awash in a halo of color. The guest chairs were placed below the desk so they had to look up into the setting sun to be responsive—a very intimidating environment, to say the least. Yes, there are exceptions to every rule.

Of course, there are those who proclaim that wearing a red tie is definitely a power play. It is true that you should carefully monitor your dress so as not to be over- or underdressed depending on the particular business marketplace in which you find yourself. Much will depend on the site of the meeting, the people in attendance, and the purpose to be served. A casual Saturday morning think tank session does not warrant a suit in most circumstances. A formal meeting in New York, San Francisco, Chicago, or Los Angeles probably would. Use your head!

Key points

- There are parameters within which the price of an item or a business is appropriate for both buyer and seller.
- Taking back a business is one of the worst alternatives in an unsuccessful sale.
- Getting the best of the other side can have serious backlash consequences.
- Negotiating is the art of adjusting your expectations.
- Misrepresentations can lead to disastrous results before and after a closing.

Worksheet

- Why should winning take a second position to fairness in any long-term sale of a business?
- What is the 10 point system?
- Why are some sales just not meant to be?
- What are some of the possible results of misrepresentations during negotiations?
- What does fast blinking mean in a negotiating session?

20

Running a Business
for Profit

It seems almost redundant to speak about "running a business for profit." After all, isn't profit the whole purpose of a business enterprise? Conceptually, this is true. It is in practice, however, that this goal of creating profit becomes obscured—for a variety of reasons. Spend a few minutes on the following exercise and you'll have an idea as to what part of the problem is.

How many people does it take to move 10 boxes 100 yards in 10 minutes? If it takes 10 people, the next questions are, what if there are 12 boxes? What if there are 20 boxes? If there are 12 boxes, it is possible that the same 10 people could move the boxes 100 yards in 10 minutes by merely working a little faster. On the other hand, if there are 20 boxes, you will probably need more people to move all the boxes 100 yards in 10 minutes. In other words, by having your people move more quickly, you can increase the output—but only up to a point. Asking them to move too quickly can cause accidents, breakage, and loss of personnel due to employee unhappiness. This basic formula applies to almost any business.

In a print shop, for example, three employees can handle monthly sales of $10,000. Those same three employees, working harder and smarter—in other words, faster—can also handle monthly sales of $20,000. With three people handling monthly sales of $10,000, the business might just about reach a break-even point—that is, there will be no profit, but neither will there be a loss. With the same three people handling monthly sales of $20,000 (and this is considered possible according to industry standards), the business might show an annual profit of $84,000. (See the chart that follows, which includes a shop doing monthly sales of $15,000 with three people.) You will note that the cost of product in percentage terms remains the same. This represents the cost of the raw material necessary to produce the product for sale. More product produced means more raw material used. The SG&A (salaries and general and administrative expenses) remains the same until the production exceeds the capacity of existing personnel or equipment or the size of the production facility—none of which would happen in the example case.

Annual Sales @ $10,000/month=	$120,000/year
Cost of Product @ 30% ($3,000/month)=	$36,000/year
SG&A @ $7,000/month=	$84,000/year
Profit	None

Annual Sales @ $15,000/month=	$180,000/year
Cost of Product @ 30% ($4,500/month)=	$54,000/year
SG&A @ $7,000/month=	$84,000/year
Profit	$42,000/year

Annual Sales @ $20,000/month=	$240,000/year
Cost of Product @ 30% ($6,000/month)=	$72,000/year
SG&A @ $7,000/month=	$84,000/year
Profit	$84,000/year

If you were the owner of this print shop, which of the above scenarios would you prefer?

Cost of product and SG&A: Another look at the rule and its exceptions

You will notice that the cost of product changes in each instance because printing requires paper and ink, the cost of which increases as more printed pages are produced. Consider that, in a shoe store, you would have to pay for each pair of shoes sold. Your cost of product in actual dollars would then be greater as you sold a greater number of shoes. You will also notice that the SG&A (salaries and general and administrative expenses) do not increase in proportion to the sales generated. This is because the rent and most other general expenses remain the same. There will, of course, be some exceptions to this.

When three people are producing $20,000/month in sales, there is likely to be overtime involved, which will increase the salaries (of the SG&A). Because people may be working later, there may be additional electricity involved, and because there are more jobs being fulfilled there may be additional costs for delivery. If these delivery charges are not reimbursed by the customer, they will become additional costs of doing business. However, the basic administrative costs do not normally change dramatically. When you get beyond the capability of the three people, you may need additional people and additional equipment. This would change the ratios and you would need to reassess your costs relative to your sales.

What about the trade-offs?

There are, of course, other considerations. At a sales level of $20,000/month, everyone is working at full capacity. There is less time for relaxation, each business hour is packed with production and, because of time pressures, there might be more errors involved in production. Errors invariably cost money. In the case of a print shop, errors could mean that jobs need to be printed a second time, which means the paper originally used is paper wasted and new paper needs to be purchased for the second printing. This increase in paper usage through error will increase the cost of product. This cost will need to be deducted from the profit produced. So, there are trade-offs.

In addition, more production means more invoices, which equates to more paperwork, more bookkeeping, and more accounting. Whether this is work done by the owner, done by an employee, or outsourced, it will certainly consume additional time—and time converts to money as an additional cost of doing business. You will not be looking at the perfect scenario in any business, but this should give you an idea as to the time/money relationship.

Three people producing $10,000/month in sales should, by comparison, leave plenty of time available, and each person should have sufficient time to produce each job perfectly and without error. But, are all of these equations correct? The answer of course, is No!

Busy people do not necessarily make more errors. People with time on their hands do not necessarily make fewer errors, nor are they likely to produce perfect jobs every time.

The fact is that two people can adequately handle $10,000/month in sales. If there are three people, one of them should be outside soliciting new customers. Three people can certainly handle $15,000/month in sales, with enough time for one person to spend some time outside soliciting new customers. With $20,000/month in sales, it is likely that all three people will be busy most of the time, and any increase in sales might suggest the hiring of a fourth person, the purchase of additional equipment, or both.

As you can see, proper use of personnel can increase the profit of a business dramatically. The same number of people can operate a business at different levels of efficiency—which means at different levels of profit. This is not true of every business. Each business has its own formulas for success and increased profitability, but it certainly is a worthwhile exercise to examine each business in terms of what costs are necessary and appropriate to properly maintain its operation.

Motivating personnel

As the owner of a business, you have plenty of incentive to work harder, longer, faster, and smarter. After all, the profit goes into your pocket. But your personnel may have different goals. Some might want to make more money. Some would prefer to leave the business on time so they can spend time with their family. Others would prefer to work at an even pace to just maintain satisfactory performance. If you are the owner, you must recognize these different goals and use them to your advantage.

Working harder should certainly equate to a bigger paycheck for those who want it. Someone who wants to spend time with his or her family might be motivated by being given vacation days during the less active periods of the business. Someone who wants to work at a particular pace may be useful in terms of creating a flexible schedule which puts his or her talents to best use during busy periods and allows him or her to be absent when the business needs are not as great.

In some cases, you may not be able to "get more out of" some people's business activities. The question is whether those people are assets to the business because they perform well at what they do or whether they should eventually be replaced by others whose performance will enhance the success potential of the business to a greater degree.

Members of the family—so to speak

Some workers are "fixtures." They have been with the business for a long time. Some customers may stay with the business because these people are still there. Some other workers are so much a part of the "family" that they are kept on because they are adequate to the tasks required of them and "adequate" is good enough in that particular job category. This is when the phrase "running a business for profit" takes on a separate meaning and is no longer a redundancy. There are many ways to keep the entire workforce content in their day-to-day activity. Gratitude for "time in grade" (an old military expression) can often work wonders as part of your employment philosophy. Don't ever completely lose sight of the people aspect of your business in favor of the profit aspect! It can often equate to dollars in strange ways.

The computer

In the history of the business marketplace there have been many innovations that have literally changed the face of business as we know it. None has been any more dynamic than the advent of the computer. It has, on the one hand, replaced many thousands of workers. It has, on the other hand, created jobs for many thousands of other workers.

The fact is—whether it increases your profit because it eliminates manual labor or increases your capacity to produce and sell because it saves time and creates more accuracy—the computer has become an integral part of the business scene.

The positive aspect of the computer is that it can enhance your business' opportunity to succeed in the marketplace. The cautionary aspect of the computer is that it was neither designed to do nor is it capable of doing everything. It is easy enough to get caught up in the concept of using the computer for just about everything. Keep in mind that the computer and its software packages have a specific shelf life, so to speak. They—both the hardware and the software—become obsolete with time. Also keep in mind that there is a learning curve involved in understanding the nuances of computer technology. It is, in a sense, a job in itself to keep up with it.

The best use of this technology is to have someone conversant with all its capabilities handling its activities. Lack of such a person, however, can hold you hostage to equipment that cannot function without its operator. This could be more detrimental to the business than the "manual time loss" it was designed to accommodate. Don't let anyone sell you the idea that "it" can do everything. To begin with, "it" does not function without an operator. Make sure that an adequate amount of "cross training" is part of your computer/personnel program!

You must make periodic judgments as to which business functions should be built into the computer. Maintaining inventory, creating price quotes, or computing and sending monthly billing are some applications that are considered "no-brainers." Do your own analysis and decide which represents time/cost savings and will not create problems in the course of your daily business activities.

Other equipment acquisition

The other aspect of the computer is that it should be examined in very much the same way you would examine the acquisition of any other piece of equipment. First of all, you must ask yourself if you have a substantial enough customer base to generate enough sales to meet the payments on the purchase of the equipment. It makes no difference whether you purchase equipment outright by borrowing from a lender (or even borrowing from yourself) or whether you lease the equipment—even with an option to purchase at the end of the lease period. You must decide if the monthly repayment schedule can be handled by the current sales picture of the company or the picture you expect to see because of the availability of the equipment you are purchasing. Be honest with yourself. Don't count on the sales if the sales are not there. There is, of course, a normal period after the initial purchase of equipment when the sales have not yet caught up with the periodic payment requirement. You must make this period as short as possible or the acquisition could prove to be a serious cost problem in the short term. Yes, there is a middle road to making this kind of decision. Getting advice from others, particularly those who have done it before you, is always a good idea. Don't rely on the sales presentation by the salesperson representing the manufacturer. Their picture will usually be something short of reality. Also, be sure to check on alternative tax situations as well before deciding on an acquisition, especially regarding whether to purchase or lease.

A more subtle aspect of replacing personnel with equipment is the effect such an acquisition might have on your people. If the acquisition will make their lives easier while increasing your profits, you will likely encounter little opposition. If, on the other hand, such an acquisition will cause a hardship in salaries or the discharge of "one of the group," you may create a situation that can cause bad feelings. Some entrepreneurs discuss some of these aspects with their employee group. Others choose not to allow the workers to participate in such a decision. Be careful you choose the right road for the right reasons.

Some quick basic reminders

Remember that most businesses are composed of four basic characteristics: 1) sales, 2) cost of product, 3) salaries and general and administrative expenses, and 4) profit. Increasing sales and decreasing costs are the bywords of the business consultant. It is unfortunate that they are not always able to share with you the method by which either of these can be accomplished.

Outside sales

It is easy to advise someone to hire a salesperson, but can the cost be accommodated by the current sales picture before the new sales—generated by this salesperson—have been included in the sales picture? Another problem with outside salespeople is that you are allowing them to have the closest relationship with your customer. If they choose to leave your employ, there is always the danger that this "control relationship" will allow them to take the customer with them—to a competitor.

Don't think that a "covenant not to compete" in a written contract is a cure for this problem. It is not enforceable in most courts, and any such litigation is costly and problematic at best. You might consider a deferred compensation plan that kicks in when they leave your employ, providing they leave the customers behind. Speak to your professional advisor about this type of "in-house insurance program." Make sure you understand the downside risk before jumping to accept advice given by someone whose livelihood does not depend on your success.

Equipment acquisition

When you buy a piece of equipment that may increase production or save time and costs, make sure you examine the monthly cost of the equipment in terms of the current sales picture. Not all new equipment will necessarily do all the things the sales representative claims it will do—and down time (when the equipment is being repaired) is time lost. Innovative equipment will oftentimes be more problematic in terms of consistency than the old "tried and true" equipment you may have been using for years. It is a good idea to retain the old equipment until the new acquisition has proven itself to be consistent in its performance.

Letting people go

It is easy enough to decide there isn't enough business to warrant keeping the workforce you have. But don't forget that the concept of business is invariably tied in with the concept of increasing sales. When sales do increase, you may be sorry you let a particular person go because you might not find someone who is as adequate to the task as the employee who is no longer there. Remember the example in the beginning of this chapter. If you have more people than your sales can currently support, take your first look at the possibility of increasing sales to warrant your current workforce. Yes, it is certainly true that, in many instances, people will have to be discharged for the sake of maintaining the continuity of the business during hard times. The hard choices are yours.

Also remember that the question of hiring additional personnel must be addressed in much the same way as the question of acquiring equipment. You must examine the cost-to-sales ratio to be sure that sales can handle the additional salary. With salespeople, there will normally be a period, sometimes lasting some months, before the efforts of the salesperson can be realized and the revenues produced are equal to or better than the advance salary this person has received. Although this is normal, be sure you anticipate this cash flow problem and have the reservoir of dollars to handle it.

No one is suggesting that the way is easy or simple. But keep in mind that the proper operation of a business does not require you to be a brain surgeon. If that were the case, most businesses would not exist in the American marketplace. You need knowledge of the particular industry, skill, careful thinking, caution (although not to a fault), discipline, and the ability to handle problems as they come along. Follow the guidelines and success will invariably be in your future.

Key points

- Understanding and working with the needs of your personnel can create a more profitable business in the long term.
- Be careful to use the computer to the best advantage of your business—but not for everything.
- Acquiring new equipment requires a serious cost-to-sales ratio analysis.
- Outside sales presents some negative aspects that must be dealt with early on.
- Make sure you properly anticipate the sales necessary to handle the payment schedule on a new piece of equipment or the hiring of additional personnel.

Worksheet

- What are some of the "trade-offs" to having your current workforce produce more product or sales?
- Why does "cost of product" change in the examples in the beginning of the chapter, whereas the costs of SG&A do not?
- Name some of the errors you can make in acquiring computer technology.
- What are some of the "no-brainers" involved in the use of computers?
- What is the purpose of a cost-to-sales ratio analysis?

21

Legal Entities:
A Simple Equation

Sole proprietorship and general partnerships

When you're deciding what form—what legal entity—your company should use to do business, don't let anyone confuse you. If you've decided to start a business by yourself—from your home or otherwise—you don't really need to use any particular legal form, like a corporation or a limited partnership. You merely have to file (in most cases) a d/b/a—"doing business as." If your name is Charles Brown and you want your company name to be CB Mfg. Co., you will file a d/b/a with your local municipal authority. It will say "Charles Brown d/b/a (doing business as) CB Mfg. Co." This will allow people who have a business relationship with CB Mfg. Co. to find out who the true owner is. They are entitled to know this and the law has created a method by which they can find out. This is the d/b/a. This is the beginning or the foundation of the relationship between you, your business, and your business community. If you are in business by yourself, your business "entity" is simply referred to as a *sole proprietorship*.

If you do business with one or more partners, and merely file a d/b/a with their names doing business as the name of your company, you would have a *simple partnership*. "Charles Brown and Alice Faye d/b/a CB Mfg. Co."

Joint and several liability

The problem with a sole proprietorship or a simple partnership, also called a general partnership, is that the owner or owners are responsible for all the financial obligations of the company. If one partner signs a contract, all the partners will be responsible. This is called *joint and several liability*. It means that any one partner can be sued for the entire obligation even if he or she is only a 10% partner, even if he or she never signed the contract—and even if he or she didn't even know about the contract. This is also true if someone sues the company for a tortious act (a tort)—like slipping on a banana peel that someone negligently left lying on the floor.

In the case of a contract, a vendor who sues the company need not be concerned about this "insider" distribution of responsibility. The outsider can sue any partner he or she chooses or may sue all the partners at the same time, and if the judgment is rendered against all the partners the outsider can actually choose the partner from whom he or she wants to collect the judgment. A partner who was not actually involved in the particular business circumstance that led to the litigation, and who can show that he or she is not responsible for the judgment, may then sue the responsible partner for reimbursement. This reimbursement, however, may come long after the "uninvolved" partner has paid the judgment to the outsider.

Corporations

The problem of liability led to the creation of a legal entity called a corporation. By forming a corporation, none of the individual owners or shareholders is liable to an outsider except under certain unique circumstances, such as fraud or misrepresentation. Such a situation allows the outsider to "pierce the corporate veil"—in other words, to break the protective shield of the corporation. Aside from these special situations, however, the corporate shield will afford the owners or shareholders, adequate protection from liability resulting from normal business activities of the corporation.

The corporate signature

Keep in mind, however, that the owners must sign all contracts with their respective "corporate signature" to maintain this protective shield. They must sign as corporate officers, for example, "Charles Brown, Vice President." If he merely signs as "Charles Brown," he is not taking advantage of the corporate protection and is acknowledging that Charles Brown, "individual," will be responsible for the corporate debt.

A good question would be, Why would a corporate officer do this? Some do it because they don't understand the difference. Some do it because many vendors and lessors will not accept a bare corporate signature. For example, in the case of a very substantial purchase or lease, the vendor or lessor may feel that the corporation's assets are not strong enough to represent solid security for the purchase. Closely held corporations and new corporations probably have just enough working capital to maintain continuity of the business. Also, most such corporations, especially new ones, don't have a lot of equity in their existing assets. Most of their assets are either on long-term lease or have been purchased with borrowed money, where the lender has usually taken an interest in the asset as security for the loan.

The security interest

In either case, the lessor or lender, having taking a down payment, will likely have taken a security interest in the assets to protect against the failure of the lessee or borrower to make the payments on the balance of the purchase price. In the event the payments are not made in accordance with the terms of such a contract or lease, the goods (if not already sold) or the equipment can be repossessed by the vendor or lessor by virtue of the security interest properly recorded.

The seller or lessor of new goods or equipment, as well as anyone lending money, recognizes that he or she cannot rely on the assets of the corporation to collect monies owed, because these assets are usually serving as security for the original purchase or lease. In such a case, these new vendors will certainly insist on a separate individual signature as a guarantee. In fact, it is likely that even the original purveyors of goods or equipment have insisted on personal signatures guaranteeing the payment in addition to the security interests they took.

The guaranty signature

This is the reason you will sometimes see two signatures on a document. One will be *"Charles Brown, Vice President"* and the second will be *"Charles Brown."* This will make Charles Brown, the individual, just as liable for the debt as the corporation, which was bound to the contract by the "Charles Brown, Vice President" signature. This should suggest to you that the corporate shield is only a limited protection. This reflects the concept of joint and several liability, allowing the creditor to seek the entire balance owed from either the corporation or the individual, or both.

Sub-chapter S corporation

The tax laws impose taxes on some corporations as if they were separate people, which, by law, the corporation actually is. This is called a "C" corporation. This tax situation differentiates it from an "S" corporation, also known as a Sub-chapter S corporation. An S corporation, contrary to the C corporation, will be taxed as if it were a general partnership, with each partner being taxed on a percentage of the corporation's profits on each of their individual tax returns. The disadvantage of an S corporation from a tax standpoint is that the individuals will be taxed on the profits of the business as their personal income—whether they actually received the profits or not.

The disadvantage of the C corporation, from a tax standpoint, is that there is a potential for a double tax. The corporation will pay a tax first on the corporate profits, and the shareholders—to whom the profits are distributed as corporate dividends—will then pay a second tax. There are reasons for this apparently inappropriate double tax, but they will not be taken up here. There are also methods by which a closely held corporation can avoid such a double taxation.

Keep in mind, however, that each corporate entity has its own advantages and disadvantages. Be sure you speak to your professional financial advisor before making a decision about which one to use.

Board of directors

Both types of corporations function with a board of directors, elected by the shareholders. The members of the board of directors may or may not be shareholders. In most small, closely held corporations, they are usually shareholders. Very often, it is a family relationship. In larger corporations, the shareholders will often choose to have a board of directors composed of people who are not shareholders. Many think this kind of group will give them a greater objectivity in helping management make business decisions.

Sometimes an individual might be invited to become a member of a board because of the particular influence he or she may have in the business or banking community that might be helpful to the company's growth. Financial people are often asked to join when management is considering the possibility of borrowing substantial sums of money or making a public offering.

Unlike shareholders—whose liability is limited to the amount of their actual investment in the company—or who may have personally guaranteed a corporate debt—the members of the board of directors have no liability to business creditors, except of course in the event they are found guilty of fraud or misrepresentation. Notwithstanding this lack of responsibility for normal business decisions, they are not immune to having lawsuits brought against them, whether such litigation is legitimate or frivolous. Serving on a board of directors has this potential for aggravation, if not responsibility. It is for this reason that many people who serve on boards will insist on having the company take out directors and officers liability insurance on their behalf. Keep in mind that even this umbrella protection will not protect either management or members of the Board from liability as the result of fraud or misrepresentation, whereas the shareholders—who may not be participating in business decisions at all—are only liable to the extent of their actual investment in the company.

Other insurance coverage

Also keep in mind that whether you are a sole proprietor, a general partner in a simple partnership, a corporation, or any other legal entity, you will always want to maintain appropriate insurance coverage for things over which you have no control. There are many times when a corporation may be sued on the basis of something having nothing to do with the business' purpose. If a customer trips on a foreign object left on the floor of the retail premises, regardless of who might have been responsible for putting it there, he or she may sue the company for negligence. If a customer is having a meal and gets sick, he or she may sue the company. This kind of collateral responsibility should always be covered by liability insurance, which is designed to handle just such a contingency.

Limited partnership

There are many variations with respect to which a particular legal entity ought to be used in any given circumstance. Each has its reason, usually because of the investors involved. For example, some investors want the protection of a corporation, but they also want one or more persons to be personally financially responsible, because most of the activity will be under that person's sole discretion. For this purpose, they may form a *"limited partnership,"* where the general partner will be totally responsible for any loss the partnership suffers, and the limited partners, just like the shareholders in a corporation, will only be responsible for the amount of their investment in the partnership.

The limited partners must be careful, however, because under this format they are not allowed to participate in the actual operation of the partnership business. If they do, they forfeit their limited partner protection and end up being treated by outsiders as just general partners. Remember the joint and several liability that applies to general partners!

Limited liability company

The above problem then led to the concept of a limited liability company, where the limited partners have no personal liability—aside from their actual investment in the company—even though they are allowed to participate in the operation of the company.

Keep in mind that, whatever legal entity you use, you must always be conscious not only of the liability issue but the tax implications as well.

Family limited liability company

The last variation of real consequence is the relatively new "family limited liability company," which is limited to a family relationship and which has, as its core investments, only family assets. This entity is particularly useful in terms of family succession of a business, because it allows periodic transfer of stock with limited tax implications.

If you have a family transition situation, you might want to examine the extent to which this is available in your particular state.

In this regard, keep in mind that there are many insurance programs that can aid in such a transition, ameliorating many otherwise onerous tax implications.

With regard to other, non-family transitions, you might want to examine the use of 401K plans, sweat equity programs, and the like. Be sure to see your professional to ensure that any such transition is handled properly.

Long-term and short-term goals

There are many purposes to be served in the creation of a business. Each goal should be carefully analyzed before making a judgment about the particular legal entity to be used. The people who put up the capital to create the business normally have the greatest influence on this decision. The nature of the business—and whether their investment is for short-term or long-term purposes—will dictate to a great degree the kind of format they will suggest.

In one case, the entrepreneur will see the operation of the business as a final goal, an instrument by which to feed the family and ultimately convert the earned equity of the business to a retirement income. In such a case, the particular legal format to be used may be of lesser importance. In another case, the group raising capital for the formation of the business may have hopes of having the business acquired by a bigger company or converting the business concept into a franchise operation. Or they may want to "take the company public." There are many goals that will cause investors to think carefully about the format they will initially use. See Chapter 7, *Franchise or Otherwise* and Chapter 10, *More on Investors and Partners*.

Other classes of stock

Some long-term goals of the investors might also include the ability to avoid certain onerous tax implications—including the "recapture" of tax savings accumulated during an early business period, or the ease by which one entity can be converted to another. This may lead to an even more sophisticated situation, where more than one class of stock is issued, where options are attached to stock certificates, or where certain classes of stock have prerogatives not given to the others. As these purposes become more evident, it should be clear that your best advice should be sought from your professionals to ensure that you make the correct decisions both for the short-term and long-term goals of the company. Be sure to talk with your professional early on!

Key points

- Don't ever lose sight of the "joint and several liability" aspect of day-to-day operations.

- The corporation can give you certain protections, but it is not designed to cover all contingencies.

- Be sure you sign all corporate documents with your "corporate signature."

- Your board of directors can serve a variety of purposes.

- Make sure you understand the short-term and long-term goals of the business early on.

Worksheet

- What can cause you to be personally liable in addition to your personal signature?

- What is the advantage of a limited partnership to you as an investor?

- What is it that you need to be careful about being a limited partner?

- What is the advantage of a sub-chapter S corporation?

- What is the disadvantage of a sub-chapter S corporation?

Index

ESTABLISH A FRAMEWORK
FOR EXCELLENCE
WITH THE OASIS PRESS®

OASIS PRESS SOFTWARE
BOOKS&
Celebrating 25 Years

THE OASIS PRESSˣ

PSI RESEARCH

P.O. BOX 3727

CENTRAL POINT, OR

97502-0032

Fastbreaking changes in technology and the global marketplace continue to create unprecedented opportunities for businesses through the '90s and into the new millennium. However with these opportunities will also come many new challenges. Today, more than ever, businesses, especially small businesses, need to excel in all areas of operation to compete and succeed in an ever-changing world.

The Successful Business Library takes you through the '90s and beyond, helping you solve the day-to-day problems you face now, and prepares you for the unexpected problems you may be facing down the road. With any of our products, you will receive up-to-date and practical business solutions, which are easy to use and easy to understand. No jargon or theories, just solid, nuts-and-bolts information.

Whether you are an entrepreneur going into business for the first time or an experienced consultant trying to keep up with the latest rules and regulations, The Successful Business Library provides you with the step-by-step guidance, and action-oriented plans you need to succeed in today's world. As an added benefit, PSI Research/The Oasis Press® unconditionally guarantees your satisfaction with the purchase of any book or software application in our catalog.

More than a marketplace for our products, we actually provide something that many business Web sites tend to overlook... useful information!

It's no mystery that the World Wide Web is a great way for businesses to promote their products, however most commercial sites stop there. We have always viewed our site's goals a little differently. For starters, we have applied our 25 years of experience providing hands-on information to small businesses directly to our Web site. We offer current information to help you start your own business, guidelines to keep it up and running, useful federal and state-specific information (including addresses and phone numbers to contact these resources), and a forum for business owners to communicate and network with others on the Internet. We would like to invite you to check out our Web site and discover the information that can assist you and your small business venture.

The Oasis Press Online
http://www.psi-research.com

From The Leading Publisher of Small Business Information
Books that save you time and money.

From The Leading Publisher of Small Business Information
Books that save you time and money.

It is projected that half of the homes in America are expected to house some type of business by the year 2000. Moonlighting takes the idea of starting your own home-based business a step further. It will show you, in realistic and achievable steps, how you can initially pursue a business dream part-time, instead of quitting your job and being without a financial safety net. This confidence building guide will help motivate you by showing you the best steps toward setting your plan in motion.

Moonlighting: Earn a Second Income at Home   **Pages: 240**
Paperback: $15.95   **ISBN: 1-55571-406-4**

An easy-to-follow guide to help you decide if starting a home-based business is right for you. Takes you on a tour of 153 home business options to start your decision process. Author David Hanania also advises potential business owners on the fiscal aspects of small startups, from financing sources to dealing with the IRS.

Home Business Made Easy   **Pages: 233**
Paperback $19.95   **ISBN: 1-55571-428-5**

A compendium of real business opportunities, not just "hot" new ventures that often have limited earning potential. *Which Business?* will help you define your skills and interests by exploring your dreams and how you think about business. Learn from profiles of 24 business areas, reviewing how each got their start and problems and successes that they have experienced.

Which Business?   **Pages: 376**
Paperback: $18.95   **ISBN: 1-55571-342-4**

If you have every wondered how to combine business success and personal signficance, author Gerald Baron has numerous practical suggestions. After years of working with executives and entrepreneurs, he's found that business success and personal meaning can share common ground. Using dozens of examples, he shows how building relationships is the key to business development and personal fulfillment.

Friendship Marketing   **Pages: 187**
Paperback $18.95   **ISBN: 1-55571-399-8**

HOW TO ORDER

Mail: Send this completed order form and a check, money order or credit card information to: PSI Research/The Oasis Press®, P.O. Box 3727, Central Point, Oregon 97502-0032

Fax: Available 24 hours a day, 7 days a week at **1-541-476-1479**

Email: info@psi-research.com (Please include a phone number, should we need to contact you.)

Web: Purchase any of our products online at our Website at **http://www.psi-research.com/oasis/**

Inquiries and International Orders: Please call 1-541-479-9464

Indicate the quantity and price of the titles you would like:

TITLE	BINDER ISBN	PAPER ISBN	BINDER	PAPERBACK	QTY.	TOTAL
Advertising Without An Agency		1-55571-429-3		☐ 19.95		
Before You Go Into Business Read This		1-55571-481-1		☐ 17.95		
Bottom Line Basics	1-55571-329-7 (B)	1-55571-330-0 (P)	☐ 39.95	☐ 19.95		
BusinessBasics		1-55571-430-7		☐ 16.95		
The Business Environmental Handbook	1-55571-304-1 (B)	1-55571-163-4 (P)	☐ 39.95	☐ 19.95		
Business Owner's Guide to Accounting and Bookkeeping		1-55571-381-5		☐ 19.95		
businessplan.com		1-55571-455-2		☐ 19.95		
Buyer's Guide to Business Insurance	1-55571-310-6 (B)	1-55571-162-6 (P)	☐ 39.95	☐ 19.95		
California Corporation Formation Package		1-55571-464-1 (P)		☐ 29.95		
Collection Techniques for a Small Business	1-55571-312-2 (B)	1-55571-171-5 (P)	☐ 39.95	☐ 19.95		
College Entrepreneur Handbook		1-55571-503-6		☐ 16.95		
A Company Policy & Personnel Workbook	1-55571-364-5 (B)	1-55571-486-2 (P)	☐ 49.95	☐ 29.95		
Company Relocation Handbook	1-55571-091-3 (B)	1-55571-092-1 (P)	☐ 39.95	☐ 19.95		
CompControl	1-55571-356-4 (B)	1-55571-355-6 (P)	☐ 39.95	☐ 19.95		
Complete Book of Business Forms		1-55571-107-3		☐ 19.95		
Connecting Online		1-55571-403-X		☐ 21.95		
Customer Engineering	1-55571-360-2 (B)	1-55571-359-9 (P)	☐ 39.95	☐ 19.95		
Delivering Legendary Customer Service		1-55571-520-6 (P)		☐ 16.95		
Develop and Market Your Creative Ideas		1-55571-383-1		☐ 15.95		
Developing International Markets		1-55571-433-1		☐ 19.95		
Doing Business in Russia		1-55571-375-0		☐ 19.95		
Draw the Line		1-55571-370-X		☐ 17.95		
The Essential Corporation Handbook		1-55571-342-4		☐ 21.95		
Essential Limited Liability Company Handbook	1-55571-362-9 (B)	1-55571-361-0 (P)	☐ 39.95	☐ 21.95		
Export Now	1-55571-192-8 (B)	1-55571-167-7 (P)	☐ 39.95	☐ 24.95		
Financial Decisionmaking		1-55571-435-8		☐ 19.95		
Financial Management Techniques	1-55571-116-2 (B)	1-55571-124-3 (P)	☐ 39.95	☐ 19.95		
Financing Your Small Business		1-55571-160-X		☐ 19.95		
Franchise Bible	1-55571-366-1 (B)	1-55571-526-5 (P)	☐ 39.95	☐ 27.95		
The Franchise Redbook		1-55571-484-6		☐ 34.95		
Friendship Marketing		1-55571-399-8		☐ 18.95		
Funding High-Tech Ventures		1-55571-405-6		☐ 21.95		
Home Business Made Easy		1-55571-428-5		☐ 19.95		
Improving Staff Productivity		1-55571-456-0		☐ 16.95		
Information Breakthrough		1-55571-413-7		☐ 22.95		
Insider's Guide to Small Business Loans		1-55571-488-9		☐ 19.95		
Keeping Score: An Inside Look at Sports Marketing		1-55571-377-7		☐ 18.95		
Kick Ass Success		1-55571-518-4		☐ 18.95		
Know Your Market	1-55571-341-6 (B)	1-55571-333-5 (P)	☐ 39.95	☐ 19.95		
Leader's Guide: 15 Essential Skills		1-55571-434-X		☐ 19.95		
Legal Expense Defense	1-55571-349-1 (B)	1-55571-348-3 (P)	☐ 39.95	☐ 19.95		
A Legal Road Map for Consultants		1-55571-460-9		☐ 18.95		
Location, Location, Location		1-55571-376-9		☐ 19.95		
Mail Order Legal Guide	1-55571-193-6 (B)	1-55571-190-1 (P)	☐ 45.00	☐ 29.95		
Managing People: A Practical Guide		1-55571-380-7		☐ 21.95		
Marketing for the New Millennium		1-55571-432-3		☐ 19.95		
Marketing Mastery	1-55571-358-0 (B)	1-55571-357-2 (P)	☐ 39.95	☐ 19.95		
Money Connection	1-55571-352-1 (B)	1-55571-351-3 (P)	☐ 39.95	☐ 24.95		
Moonlighting: Earning a Second Income at Home		1-55571-406-4		☐ 15.95		
Navigating the Marketplace: Growth Strategies for Small Business		1-55571-458-7		☐ 21.95		
No Money Down Financing for Franchising		1-55571-462-5		☐ 19.95		
Not Another Meeting!		1-55571-480-3		☐ 17.95		
People-Centered Profit Strategies		1-55571-517-6		☐ 18.95		
				Sub-total for this side:		

TITLE		ISBN	BINDER	PAPERBACK	QTY.	TOTAL
People Investment	1-55571-187-1 (B)	1-55571-161-8 (P)	☐ 39.95	☐ 19.95		
Power Marketing for Small Business		1-55571-524-9 (P)		☐ 19.95		
Proposal Development	1-55571-067-0 (B)	1-55571-431-5 (P)	☐ 39.95	☐ 21.95		
Prospecting for Gold		1-55571-483-8		☐ 14.95		
Public Relations Marketing		1-55571-459-5		☐ 19.95		
Raising Capital	1-55571-306-8 (B)	1-55571-305-X (P)	☐ 39.95	☐ 19.95		
Renaissance 2000		1-55571-412-9		☐ 22.95		
Retail in Detail		1-55571-371-8		☐ 15.95		
The Rule Book of Business Plans for Startups		1-55571-519-2		☐ 18.95		
Secrets of High Ticket Selling		1-55571-436-6		☐ 19.95		
Secrets to Buying and Selling a Business		1-55571-489-7		☐ 24.95		
Secure Your Future		1-55571-335-1		☐ 19.95		
Selling Services		1-55571-461-7		☐ 14.95		
SmartStart Your (State) Business		varies per state		☐ 19.95		
Indicate which state you prefer:						
Small Business Insider's Guide to Bankers		1-55571-400-5		☐ 18.95		
Start Your Business		1-55571-485-4		☐ 10.95		
Strategic Insights		1-55571-505-2		☐ 19.95		
Strategic Management for Small and Growing Firms		1-55571-465-X		☐ 24.95		
Successful Network Marketing		1-55571-350-5		☐ 15.95		
Surviving Success		1-55571-446-3		☐ 19.95		
TargetSmart!		1-55571-384-X		☐ 19.95		
Top Tax Saving Ideas for Today's Small Business		1-55571-463-3		☐ 16.95		
Truth About Teams		1-55571-482-X		☐ 18.95		
Twenty-One Sales in a Sale		1-55571-448-X		☐ 19.95		
WebWise	1-55571-501-X (B)	1-55571-479-X (P)	☐ 29.95	☐ 19.95		
What's It Worth?		1-55571-504-4		☐ 22.95		
Which Business?		1-55571-390-4		☐ 18.95		
Write Your Own Business Contracts	1-55571-196-0 (B)	1-55571-487-0 (P)	☐ 39.95	☐ 24.95		

Success Series	ISBN	PAPERBACK	QTY.	TOTAL
50 Ways to Get Promoted	1-55571-506-0	☐ 10.95		
You Can't Go Wrong By Doing It Right	1-55571-490-0	☐ 14.95		

Oasis Software	FORMAT	BINDER	PAPERBACK	QTY.	TOTAL
Company Policy Text Files CD-ROM	CD-ROM ☐		☐ 49.95		
Company Policy Text Files Book & CD-ROM Package	CD-ROM ☐	☐ 89.95 (B)	☐ 69.95 (P)		
Winning Business Plans in Color CD-ROM	CD-ROM ☐		☐ 59.95		

Subtotal from other side	
Subtotal from this side	
▶ Shipping	
TOTAL	

Ordered by: *Please give street address*

NAME   TITLE

COMPANY

STREET ADDRESS

CITY   STATE   ZIP

DAYTIME PHONE   EMAIL

Ship to: *If different than above*

NAME   TITLE

COMPANY

STREET ADDRESS

CITY   STATE   ZIP

DAYTIME PHONE

Shipping:

YOUR ORDER IS:	ADD:
0-25	5.00
25.01-50	6.00
50.01-100	7.00
100.01-175	9.00
175.01-250	13.00
250.01-500	18.00
500.01+	4% of total

PLEASE CALL FOR RUSH SERVICE OPTIONS.
INTERNATIONAL ORDERS, PLEASE CALL FOR A QUOTE ON CURRENT SHIPPING RATES.

Payment Method:
☐ CHECK   ☐ MONEY ORDER
☐ AMERICAN EXPRESS ☐ DISCOVER
☐ MASTERCARD   ☐ VISA

CREDIT CARD NUMBER

EXPIRATION (MM/YY)   NAME ON CARD (PLEASE PRINT)

SIGNATURE OF CARDHOLDER (REQUIRED)

Fax this order form to: (541) 476-1479 or mail it to: P.O. Box 3727, Central Point, Oregon 97502
For more information about our products or to order online, visit http://www.psi-research.com

OASIS PRESS BOOKS & SOFTWARE